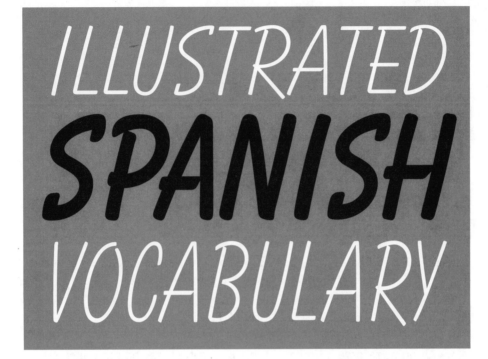

ILLUSTRATED SPANISH VOCABULARY

FALL RIVER PRESS

New York

FALL RIVER PRESS

New York

An Imprint of Sterling Publishing
387 Park Avenue South
New York, NY 10016

Cover designed by Igor Satanovsky
Illustrations by Dan O. Williams

ISBN 978-1-4351-4708-9

For information about custom editions, special sales, and premium and corporate purchases, please contact Sterling Special Sales at 800-805-5489 or specialsales@sterlingpublishing.com.

Manufactured in Canada

2   4   6   8   10   9   7   5   3   1

www.sterlingpublishing.com

Acknowledgments

Many people at SparkNotes helped to make this book possible and (we hope you agree) great. Lindsay Weiskittel, our tireless editor, provided patient feedback and wrangled our sentences and schedules with aplomb. We are grateful for her hard work and dedication. Our many thanks go out to Laurie Barnett for pitching us this idea in the first place, and for showing us the publishing ropes. Liz Kessler's investigative skills and sharp wit have been invaluable. Thanks to Alysha Bullock for final shepherding.

We must also offer a hearty thank you to our families in Arizona and New York, who supported and encouraged us as we worked together in life and on the page.

Contents

Introduction

When learning a new language, building a large vocabulary is essential. It not only allows you to communicate more effectively and accurately but also makes you sound more polished and sophisticated. A high-level vocabulary makes you sound less like a novice and more like a native speaker. More important, it can raise your score on Spanish-language exams.

Whatever your reason for wanting to expand your Spanish vocabulary, this book can help. You'll walk away having learned and memorized 250 key verbs, adjectives, and adverbs—and you'll have done it painlessly. You might even have some fun! And it's all because of the power of mnemonics.

What's a Mnemonic?

Mnemonic (nuh-MON-ik) is just a fancy way of saying "memory aid." A mnemonic usually takes the form of a short, easily memorized saying. You probably already use several of them in your daily life. Play an instrument? You might have learned the musical scale by memorizing this handy saying: **E**very **G**ood **B**oy **D**eserves **F**un. Maybe you mutter "righty-tighty, lefty-loosey" whenever you have to fix something with a wrench, or maybe you recite "*I* before *E* except after *C* " whenever you have to spell *receive* or *believe*. These are all examples of common mnemonics. (Try saying that ten times fast!)

The Power of Mnemonics

We created this book because we felt there should be an easier, more fun way to learn Spanish vocabulary. Because let's face it: Life is too short to sit around memorizing word lists! We started with 250 of the most important and frequently used Spanish words. Then we created a unique, mnemonics-based learning system around those words to help you learn and truly memorize their meanings. We use a variety of components to make these new words and their definitions stick: everything from rhythm and rhyme to humor and dynamic illustrations. So now, studying vocab won't just be more effective—it'll actually be fun!

Ride the power of mnemonics to a better, stronger Spanish vocabulary with *Illustrated Spanish Vocabulary*.

How to Use This Book

This book uses multiple tactics to help you understand, learn, and memorize 250 key Spanish words. Each page has five components that work in concert to make sure each new word sticks—and sticks firmly.

1. The Vocabulary Word, including its pronunciation, part of speech, and definition.

creer cre-ER (*v.*) to believe

2. The Mnemonic Phrase, a rhyming sentence that includes the English sound link and a reminder of the Spanish word's definition. Don't blame us if you start walking around the house chanting these sentences to yourself—that's the point! They're sing-songy and silly so you remember them easily.

The tribal chiefs had _creepy beliefs_.

3. The Sound Links, familiar English words or phrases that sound like the Spanish vocabulary word. Each sound link rhymes with the vocabulary word and uses sound similarities.

creer (Spanish) . . .
creepy (English)

4. The Illustration drives the mnemonic home. If you're a better visual learner than you are an auditory learner (that is, someone who learns through sounds), the illustration will help trigger your memory when you have to recall the word's definition.

5. Verb conjugations also appear when appropriate. We give you conjugations in the present and simple, past indicative mood (the preterite) for each of the 150 Spanish verbs in this book.

PRESENT TENSE	
Yo	creo
Tú	crees
Él/Ella/Ud.	cree
Nosotros	creemos
Vosotros	creéis
Ellos/Ellas/Uds.	creen

PRETERITE TENSE	
Yo	creí
Tú	creíste
Él/Ella/Ud.	creyó
Nosotros	creímos
Vosotros	creísteis
Ellos/Ellas/Uds.	creyeron

You can flip through this book randomly, stopping at pages that catch your eye and learning the words on that page. But if you want to be more disciplined about it—if you're bulking up your vocab for a test, for example—work through the words in the order they're presented. After every group of ten words, you'll see the following two drills:

1. **Refresh Your Memory.** Here you'll match the term with the correct definition.
2. **Test Your Knowledge.** This drill is a series of fill-in-the-blank sentences.

After working through a set of words, try one of the exercises. Score well? Try the next one. Score lower than you'd like? Go back and review the words in question, then test yourself again with the second exercise.

However you decide to use this book, you're sure to end up with a wider, more sophisticated Spanish vocabulary. So what are you waiting for? Turn the page and start memorizing with mnemonics!

VERBS

tomar

to-MAR (*v.*): to take

What would it *take*
to mar this beautiful cake?

PRESENT TENSE		PRETERITE TENSE	
Yo	**tomo**	Yo	**tomé**
Tú	**tomas**	Tú	**tomaste**
Él/Ella/Ud.	**toma**	Él/Ella/Ud.	**tomó**
Nosotros	**tomamos**	Nosotros	**tomamos**
Vosotros	**tomáis**	Vosotros	**tomasteis**
Ellos/Ellas/Uds.	**toman**	Ellos/Ellas/Uds.	**tomaron**

esperar

e-spe-RAR **(v.):** to hope for; to wait

Tired Mrs. Tink
hopes **for an** *espresso* **drink.**

PRESENT TENSE		PRETERITE TENSE	
Yo	**espero**	Yo	**esperé**
Tú	**esperas**	Tú	**eseraste**
Él/Ella/Ud.	**espera**	Él/Ella/Ud.	**esperó**
Nosotros	**esperamos**	Nosotros	**esperamos**
Vosotros	**esperáis**	Vosotros	**esperasteis**
Ellos/Ellas/Uds.	**esperan**	Ellos/Ellas/Uds.	**esperaron**

estudiar

e-stoo-dee-AR (*v.*): to study

Studious *students study* with their studious student buddies.

PRESENT TENSE		PRETERITE TENSE	
Yo	estudio	Yo	estudié
Tú	estudias	Tú	estudiaste
Él/Ella/Ud.	estudia	Él/Ella/Ud.	estudió
Nosotros	estudiamos	Nosotros	estudiamos
Vosotros	estudiáis	Vosotros	estudiasteis
Ellos/Ellas/Uds.	estudian	Ellos/Ellas/Uds.	estudiaron

dibujar

dee-boo-HAR (*v.*): to draw, sketch

**The *boo* he *drew*
wouldn't *jar* a girl of two.**

PRESENT TENSE		PRETERITE TENSE	
Yo	dibujo	Yo	dibujé
Tú	dibujas	Tú	dibujaste
Él/Ella/Ud.	dibuja	Él/Ella/Ud.	dibujó
Nosotros	dibujamos	Nosotros	dibujamos
Vosotros	dibujáis	Vosotros	dibujasteis
Ellos/Ellas/Uds.	dibujan	Ellos/Ellas/Uds.	dibujaron

regresar

re-gre-SAR (): to return

**When Reggie *regresses*,
he *returns* to his messes.**

PRESENT TENSE		PRETERITE TENSE	
Yo	**regreso**	Yo	**regresé**
Tú	**regresa**	Tú	**regresaste**
Él/Ella/Ud.	**regresas**	Él/Ella/Ud.	**regresó**
Nosotros	**regresamos**	Nosotros	**regresamos**
Vosotros	**regresaías**	Vosotros	**regresasteis**
Ellos/Ellas/Uds.	**regresan**	Ellos/Ellas/Uds.	**regresaron**

buscar

boo-SKAR (**v.**): to look for

In a *bus* or in a *car*,
the talent scout always *looks* for a star.

PRESENT TENSE		PRETERITE TENSE	
Yo	busco	Yo	busqué
Tú	buscas	Tú	buscaste
Él/Ella/Ud.	busca	Él/Ella/Ud.	buscó
Nosotros	buscamos	Nosotros	buscamos
Vosotros	buscáis	Vosotros	buscasteis
Ellos/Ellas/Uds.	buscan	Ellos/Ellas/Uds.	buscaron

escribir

e-skree-BEER (*v.*): to write

Hester McBibble
writes **her signature like a** *scribble*.

PRESENT TENSE		PRETERITE TENSE	
Yo	escribo	Yo	escribí
Tú	escribes	Tú	escribiste
Él/Ella/Ud.	escribe	Él/Ella/Ud.	escribió
Nosotros	escribimos	Nosotros	escribimos
Vosotros	escribís	Vosotros	escribisteis
Ellos/Ellas/Uds.	escriben	Ellos/Ellas/Uds.	escribieron

creer

cre-ER **(v.)**: to believe

The tribal chiefs had _creepy_ beliefs.

PRESENT TENSE		PRETERITE TENSE	
Yo	creo	Yo	creí
Tú	crees	Tú	creíste
Él/Ella/Ud.	cree	Él/Ella/Ud.	creyó
Nosotros	creemos	Nosotros	creímos
Vosotros	creéis	Vosotros	creísteis
Ellos/Ellas/Uds.	creen	Ellos/Ellas/Uds.	creyeron

aprender

a-pren-DER (*v.*): to learn

The menaced *apprentice*
learns to be a dentist.

PRESENT TENSE		PRETERITE TENSE	
Yo	aprendo	Yo	aprendí
Tú	aprendes	Tú	aprendiste
Él/Ella/Ud.	aprende	Él/Ella/Ud.	aprendió
Nosotros	aprendemos	Nosotros	aprendimos
Vosotros	aprendéis	Vosotros	aprendisteis
Ellos/Ellas/Uds.	aprenden	Ellos/Ellas/Uds.	aprendieron

vender

ven-DER (*v.*): to sell

The mustachioed *vender* sells bonnets for beautiful belles.

PRESENT TENSE		PRETERITE TENSE	
Yo	vendo	Yo	vendí
Tú	vendes	Tú	vendiste
Él/Ella/Ud.	vende	Él/Ella/Ud.	vendió
Nosotros	vendemos	Nosotros	vendimos
Vosotros	vendéis	Vosotros	vendisteis
Ellos/Ellas/Uds.	venden	Ellos/Ellas/Uds.	vendieron

DRILL 1

Refresh Your Memory

Match the word and link to its corresponding definition.

1. tomar (to mar) E.
2. esperar (espresso) A.
3. estudiar (students) G.
4. dibujar (boo … jar) H.
5. regresar (regresses) C.
6. buscar (bus … car) I.
7. escribir (scribble) B.
8. creer (creepy) J.
9. aprender (apprentice) F.
10. vender (vender) D.

A. to hope for
B. to write
C. to return
D. to sell
E. to take
F. to learn
G. to study
H. to draw, sketch
I. to look for
J. to believe

Test Your Knowledge

Fill in the blanks with the present tense of the appropriate verb, except where indicated.

1. Yo _espero_ viajar a España este verano, pero no sé si tendré tiempo.
2. Yo quisiera ser artista, pero no _dibujo_ bien.
3. Cuando estabas enfermo, _tomaste_ [preterite] una medicina muy fuerte.
4. ¿Cuándo _____ [preterite] tú y Damián de vuestro viaje?
5. Mi hermano _____ un apartamento de dos dormitorios.
6. Este verano voy a _aprender_ a manejar. Quiero sacar la licencia.
7. Margarita, ¿ _estudiaste_ [preterite] para el examen?
8. Miguel Cervantes _escribió_ [preterite] el libro Don Quijote de la Mancha.
9. Jaime, ¿_____ en Dios?
10. El señor López nos _____ [preterite] un reloj muy fino.

16

leer

le-ER **(*v.*):** to read

**Instead of _leering_ at the cute girl in class,
he'd finally *read* the book—much less crass.**

PRESENT TENSE		PRETERITE TENSE	
Yo	leo	Yo	leí
Tú	lees	Tú	leíste
Él/Ella/Ud.	lee	Él/Ella/Ud.	leyó
Nosotros	leemos	Nosotros	leímos
Vosotros	leéis	Vosotros	leísteis
Ellos/Ellas/Uds.	leen	Ellos/Ellas/Uds.	leyeron

comer

ko-MER (*v.*): to eat

**Crushed-out Sandy and her sweetheart Pete
meet on the _corner to eat_ a sweet treat.**

PRESENT TENSE		PRETERITE TENSE	
Yo	**como**	Yo	**comí**
Tú	**comes**	Tú	**comiste**
Él/Ella/Ud.	**come**	Él/Ella/Ud.	**comió**
Nosotros	**comemos**	Nosotros	**comimos**
Vosotros	**coméis**	Vosotros	**comisteis**
Ellos/Ellas/Uds.	**comen**	Ellos/Ellas/Uds.	**comieron**

mirar

mee-RAR (*v.*): to look

**Stylish Mirah shed a tear
when she *looked* at her new 'do in the _mirror_.**

PRESENT TENSE		PRETERITE TENSE	
Yo	miro	Yo	miré
Tú	miras	Tú	miraste
Él/Ella/Ud.	mira	Él/Ella/Ud.	miró
Nosotros	miramos	Nosotros	miramos
Vosotros	miráis	Vosotros	mirasteis
Ellos/Ellas/Uds.	miran	Ellos/Ellas/Uds.	miraron

abrir

a-BREER (*v.*): to open

**Honey, would you be a dear
and *open* the fridge and bring me *a beer*?**

PRESENT TENSE		PRETERITE TENSE	
Yo	**abro**	Yo	**abrí**
Tú	**abres**	Tú	**abriste**
Él/Ella/Ud.	**abre**	Él/Ella/Ud.	**abrió**
Nosotros	**abrimos**	Nosotros	**abrimos**
Vosotros	**abrís**	Vosotros	**abristeis**
Ellos/Ellas/Uds.	**abren**	Ellos/Ellas/Uds.	**abrieron**

vivir

vee-VEER (*v.*): to live, exist

**Don't come to Alaska and our icy river;
if you're going *to live* here, you're going to *shiver*.**

PRESENT TENSE		PRETERITE TENSE	
Yo	**vivo**	Yo	**viví**
Tú	**vives**	Tú	**viviste**
Él/Ella/Ud.	**vive**	Él/Ella/Ud.	**vivió**
Nosotros	**vivimos**	Nosotros	**vivimos**
Vosotros	**vivís**	Vosotros	**vivisteis**
Ellos/Ellas/Uds.	**viven**	Ellos/Ellas/Uds.	**vivieron**

pensar

pen-SAR (*v.*): to think

Farmer Jen *thinks* her rickety chicken <u>pens</u> <u>are</u> going to hold her boisterous hen.

PRESENT TENSE		PRETERITE TENSE	
Yo	**pienso**	Yo	**pensé**
Tú	**piensas**	Tú	**pensaste**
Él/Ella/Ud.	**piensa**	Él/Ella/Ud.	**pensó**
Nosotros	**pensamos**	Nosotros	**pensamos**
Vosotros	**pensáis**	Vosotros	**pensasteis**
Ellos/Ellas/Uds.	**piensan**	Ellos/Ellas/Uds.	**pensaron**

entender

en-ten-DER (*v.*): to understand

Gwen *intends to understand* men:
Her Dating 101 class will ensure
she doesn't end up an old hen.

PRESENT TENSE		PRETERITE TENSE	
Yo	entiendo	Yo	entendí
Tú	entiendes	Tú	entendiste
Él/Ella/Ud.	entiende	Él/Ella/Ud.	entendió
Nosotros	entendemos	Nosotros	entendimos
Vosotros	entendéis	Vosotros	entendisteis
Ellos/Ellas/Uds.	entienden	Ellos/Ellas/Uds.	entendieron

mentir

men-TEER (*v.*): to lie, deceive

If you promise beer and *lie*,
***men tear* up and really cry.**

PRESENT TENSE		PRETERITE TENSE	
Yo	miento	Yo	mentí
Tú	mientes	Tú	mentiste
Él/Ella/Ud.	miente	Él/Ella/Ud.	mintió
Nosotros	mentimos	Nosotros	mentimos
Vosotros	mentís	Vosotros	mentisteis
Ellos/Ellas/Uds.	mienten	Ellos/Ellas/Uds.	mintieron

traer

tra-ER (*v.*): to bring, wear

Tom *brings* his spare parts to *Trader* Bart's.

PRESENT TENSE		PRETERITE TENSE	
Yo	traigo	Yo	traje
Tú	traes	Tú	trajiste
Él/Ella/Ud.	trae	Él/Ella/Ud.	trajo
Nosotros	traemos	Nosotros	trajimos
Vosotros	traéis	Vosotros	trajisteis
Ellos/Ellas/Uds.	traen	Ellos/Ellas/Uds.	trajeron

poner

po-NER (*v.*): to put

"*Pony* up!" says Mabel.
"*Put* your bets on the table!"

PRESENT TENSE		PRETERITE TENSE	
Yo	pongo	Yo	puse
Tú	pones	Tú	pusiste
Él/Ella/Ud.	pone	Él/Ella/Ud.	puso
Nosotros	ponemos	Nosotros	pusimos
Vosotros	ponéis	Vosotros	pusisteis
Ellos/Ellas/Uds.	ponen	Ellos/Ellas/Uds.	pusieron

DRILL 2

Refresh Your Memory

Match the word and link to its corresponding definition.

1. leer (leering)
2. comer (corner)
3. mirar (mirror)
4. abrir (a beer)
5. vivir (shiver)
6. pensar (pens are)
7. entender (intends)
8. mentir (men tear)
9. traer (Trader)
10. poner (pony)

A. to live, exist
B. to read
C. to lie, deceive
D. to understand
E. to look
F. to put
G. to bring, wear
H. to eat
I. to open
J. to think

Test Your Knowledge

Fill in the blanks with the present tense of the appropriate verb, except where indicated.

1. Si necesitas alguna cosa, yo te la _____ en seguida.

2. ¿Qué _____ por la ventana, Julieta?

3. De joven, su abuelo _____ [preterite] dos años en Nueva York.

4. El año pasado los estudiantes _____ [preterite] el libro La Celestina.

5. Para la cena, nosotros _____ [preterite] pescado frito con ensalada.

6. Magdalena y Juan Carlos, ¿qué _____ hacer esta tarde?

7. Muchachos, ¿_____ [preterite] las instrucciones de la profesora?

8. Cuando llego a casa, siempre _____ todas las ventanas.

9. A veces los niños _____ porque tienen miedo de decir la verdad.

10. Mamá, ¿dónde _____ [preterite] mi mochila?

salir

sa-LEER (*v.*): to leave

As the beautiful twins *leave* with their beers, <u>*Sal leers*</u> at their pretty rears.

PRESENT TENSE		PRETERITE TENSE	
Yo	**salgo**	Yo	**salí**
Tú	**sales**	Tú	**saliste**
Él/Ella/Ud.	**sale**	Él/Ella/Ud.	**salió**
Nosotros	**salimos**	Nosotros	**salimos**
Vosotros	**salís**	Vosotros	**salisteis**
Ellos/Ellas/Uds.	**salen**	Ellos/Ellas/Uds.	**salieron**

decir

de-SEER (*v.*): to say, tell

**The teachers in the hallway *say*, plain and clear,
"You really can't play with *dice* in *here*!"**

PRESENT TENSE	
Yo	digo
Tú	dices
Él/Ella/Ud.	dice
Nosotros	decimos
Vosotros	decís
Ellos/Ellas/Uds.	dicen

PRETERITE TENSE	
Yo	dije
Tú	dijiste
Él/Ella/Ud.	dijo
Nosotros	dijimos
Vosotros	dijisteis
Ellos/Ellas/Uds.	dijeron

dar

dar (*v.*): to give

Darling, *give* me your hand,
or else I'll be stuck in this darn sand!

PRESENT TENSE		PRETERITE TENSE	
Yo	doy	Yo	di
Tú	das	Tú	diste
Él/Ella/Ud.	da	Él/Ella/Ud.	dio
Nosotros	damos	Nosotros	dimos
Vosotros	dais	Vosotros	disteis
Ellos/Ellas/Uds.	dan	Ellos/Ellas/Uds.	dieron

confiar

kon-fee-AR (*v.*): to trust

This _cone's fear_ is the ice cream scoop,
but he *trusts* the other cone friends in his group.

PRESENT TENSE		PRETERITE TENSE	
Yo	**confío**	Yo	**confié**
Tú	**confías**	Tú	**confiaste**
Él/Ella/Ud.	**confía**	Él/Ella/Ud.	**confió**
Nosotros	**confiamos**	Nosotros	**confiamos**
Vosotros	**confiáis**	Vosotros	**confiasteis**
Ellos/Ellas/Uds.	**confían**	Ellos/Ellas/Uds.	**confiaron**

ser

ser (*v.*): is (to be)

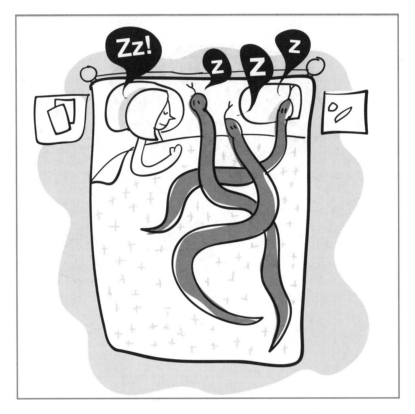

**Sara's *serpents* *are* red,
and strangely enough, they sleep in her bed.**

PRESENT TENSE		PRETERITE TENSE	
Yo	soy	Yo	fui
Tú	eres	Tú	fuiste
Él/Ella/Ud.	es	Él/Ella/Ud.	fue
Nosotros	somos	Nosotros	fuimos
Vosotros	sois	Vosotros	fuisteis
Ellos/Ellas/Uds.	son	Ellos/Ellas/Uds.	fueron

estar

e-STAR (*v.*): is (to be)

**Esther *is <u>a star</u>* on her own bed,
performing for her brother in her gown of red.**

PRESENT TENSE		PRETERITE TENSE	
Yo	estoy	Yo	estuve
Tú	estás	Tú	estuviste
Él/Ella/Ud.	está	Él/Ella/Ud.	estuvo
Nosotros	estamos	Nosotros	estuvimos
Vosotros	estáis	Vosotros	estuvisteis
Ellos/Ellas/Uds.	están	Ellos/Ellas/Uds.	estuvieron

despertarse

de-sper-TAR-se **(*v.*): to wake up**

Desperate **Kareem** *woke* **from a bad dream—
one in which he busted at the seam.**

PRESENT TENSE		PRETERITE TENSE	
Yo	**me despierto**	Yo	**me desperté**
Tú	**te despiertas**	Tú	**te despertaste**
Él/Ella/Ud.	**se despierta**	Él/Ella/Ud.	**se despertó**
Nosotros	**nos despertamos**	Nosotros	**nos despertamos**
Vosotros	**os despertáis**	Vosotros	**os despertasteis**
Ellos/Ellas/Uds.	**se despiertan**	Ellos/Ellas/Uds.	**se despertaron**

bañarse

ba–NYAR–se (*v.*): to bathe

Bathing is *banned*
across all Filthyland.

PRESENT TENSE		PRETERITE TENSE	
Yo	me baño	Yo	me bañé
Tú	te bañas	Tú	te bañaste
Él/Ella/Ud.	se baña	Él/Ella/Ud.	se bañó
Nosotros	nos bañamos	Nosotros	nos bañamos
Vosotros	os bañáis	Vosotros	os bañasteis
Ellos/Ellas/Uds.	se bañan	Ellos/Ellas/Uds.	se bañaron

levantar

le–van–TAR (*v.*): to raise, lift

The spell to *levitate*, or *to raise*, put the sorceress in a daze.

PRESENT TENSE		PRETERITE TENSE	
Yo	me levanto	Yo	me levanté
Tú	te levantas	Tú	te levantaste
Él/Ella/Ud.	se levanta	Él/Ella/Ud.	se levantó
Nosotros	nos levantamos	Nosotros	nos levantamos
Vosotros	os levantáis	Vosotros	os levantasteis
Ellos/Ellas/Uds.	se levantan	Ellos/Ellas/Uds.	se levantaron

lavarse

la–VAR–se (*v.*): to wash

**Torrie always *washes*
lava off her galoshes.**

PRESENT TENSE		PRETERITE TENSE	
Yo	me lavo	Yo	me lavé
Tú	te lavas	Tú	te lavaste
Él/Ella/Ud.	se lava	Él/Ella/Ud.	se lavó
Nosotros	nos lavamos	Nosotros	nos lavamos
Vosotros	os laváis	Vosotros	os lavasteis
Ellos/Ellas/Uds.	se lavan	Ellos/Ellas/Uds.	se lavaron

DRILL 3

Refresh Your Memory

Match the word and link to its corresponding definition.

1. salir (Sal leers)
2. decir (dice ... here)
3. dar (darling)
4. confiar (cone's fear)
5. ser (serpents)
6. estar (a star)
7. despertarse (desperate)
8. bañarse (banned)
9. levantar (levitate)
10. lavarse (lava)

A. to trust
B. to raise, lift
C. to say, tell
D. is (to be) [description]
E. to bathe
F. to give
G. to wash
H. to leave
I. to wake up
J. is (to be) [location]

Test Your Knowledge

Fill in the blanks with the present tense of the appropriate verb, except where indicated.

1. Javier, ¿le _____ [preterite] tu pasaje a la azafata?

2. Pasaron la tarde en la lavandería _____ [preterite] toda la ropa sucia.

3. La señora nos _____ [preterite] que no quería ir a sala de emergencias.

4. Necesito un nuevo doctor: no _____ en el que tengo actualmente.

5. Yo y Francisca _____ estudiando en la sala.

6. Los viernes nosotros _____ de casa a las nueve de la noche.

7. Esta mañana yo _____ [preterite] tarde: estaba agotado por falta de sueño la noche anterior.

8. Hoy no _____ [preterite] los chicos: no había agua caliente.

9. Marta _____ mi mejor amiga.

10. ¿Me ayudas a _____ esta caja? Está muy pesada.

sentarse

sen-tar-se (*v.*): to sit down

**The lazy _centaur_ sits down
in the center of town.**

PRESENT TENSE		PRETERITE TENSE	
Yo	me siento	Yo	me senté
Tú	te sientas	Tú	te sentaste
Él/Ella/Ud.	se sienta	Él/Ella/Ud.	se sentó
Nosotros	nos sentamos	Nosotros	nos sentamos
Vosotros	os sentáis	Vosotros	os sentasteis
Ellos/Ellas/Uds.	se sientan	Ellos/Ellas/Uds.	se sentaron

resfriarse

res-free-AR-se (*v.*): to catch a cold

Rest, Friar, you *say* you're getting old;
if you go outside now, you'll *catch a cold*.

PRESENT TENSE		PRETERITE TENSE	
Yo	me resfrío	Yo	me resfrié
Tú	te resfrías	Tú	te resfriaste
Él/Ella/Ud.	se resfría	Él/Ella/Ud.	se resfrió
Nosotros	nos resfriamos	Nosotros	nos resfriamos
Vosotros	os resfriáis	Vosotros	os resfriasteis
Ellos/Ellas/Uds.	se resfrían	Ellos/Ellas/Uds.	se resfriaron

casarse

ka-SAR-se **(v.):** to marry

"*Cars are*," *says* Paul, "a way to know
if the girl you'll *marry* has got some dough."

PRESENT TENSE		PRETERITE TENSE	
Yo	me caso	Yo	me casé
Tú	te casas	Tú	te casaste
Él/Ella/Ud.	se casa	Él/Ella/Ud.	se casó
Nosotros	nos casamos	Nosotros	nos casamos
Vosotros	os casáis	Vosotros	os casasteis
Ellos/Ellas/Uds.	se casan	Ellos/Ellas/Uds.	se casaron

atreverse

a-tre-VER-se **(v.)**: to dare

"Ah, Trevor," *says* Doug, "I've got a *dare*:
go tug on that lever over there."

PRESENT TENSE		PRETERITE TENSE	
Yo	me atrevo	Yo	me atreví
Tú	te atreves	Tú	te atreviste
Él/Ella/Ud.	se atreve	Él/Ella/Ud.	se atrevió
Nosotros	nos atrevemos	Nosotros	nos atrevimos
Vosotros	os atrevéis	Vosotros	os atrevisteis
Ellos/Ellas/Uds.	se atreven	Ellos/Ellas/Uds.	se atrevieron

asustarse

a-soo-STAR-se **(v.): to scare**

**"You should _sue the star_," _says_ lawyer Jim,
"you'll _scare_ some money out of him."**

PRESENT TENSE		PRETERITE TENSE	
Yo	me asusto	Yo	me asusté
Tú	te asustas	Tú	te asustaste
Él/Ella/Ud.	se asusta	Él/Ella/Ud.	se asustó
Nosotros	nos asustamos	Nosotros	nos asustó
Vosotros	os asustáis	Vosotros	os asustasteis
Ellos/Ellas/Uds.	se asustan	Ellos/Ellas/Uds.	se asustaron

enfadarse

en–fa–DAR–se (*v.*): to anger, annoy

**The annoying ringtone _fad_ angered Chad,
who _says_ he normally doesn't get so very mad.**

PRESENT TENSE		PRETERITE TENSE	
Yo	me enfado	Yo	me enfadé
Tú	te enfadas	Tú	te enfadaste
Él/Ella/Ud.	se enfada	Él/Ella/Ud.	se enfadó
Nosotros	nos enfadamos	Nosotros	nos enfadamos
Vosotros	os enfadáis	Vosotros	os enfadasteis
Ellos/Ellas/Uds.	se enfadan	Ellos/Ellas/Uds.	se enfadaron

reírse

re-EER-se (*v.*): to laugh

**The grouchy old ladies in the _rear say_
it's not nice to _laugh_ at hearsay.**

PRESENT TENSE		PRETERITE TENSE	
Yo	me río	Yo	me reí
Tú	te ríes	Tú	te reíste
Él/Ella/Ud.	se ríe	Él/Ella/Ud.	se rió
Nosotros	nos reímos	Nosotros	nos reímos
Vosotros	os reís	Vosotros	os reísteis
Ellos/Ellas/Uds.	se ríen	Ellos/Ellas/Uds.	se rieron

llegar

ye-GAR (*v.*): to arrive

"Yay, you've *arrived*!"
said *Hagar* to baby number five.

PRESENT TENSE		PRETERITE TENSE	
Yo	llego	Yo	llegué
Tú	llegas	Tú	llegaste
Él/Ella/Ud.	llega	Él/Ella/Ud.	llegó
Nosotros	llegamos	Nosotros	llegamos
Vosotros	llegáis	Vosotros	llegasteis
Ellos/Ellas/Uds.	llegan	Ellos/Ellas/Uds.	llegaron

viajar

vya-HAR (*v.*): to travel

**The firefly *traveled via jar*,
but it certainly didn't get very far.**

PRESENT TENSE		PRETERITE TENSE	
Yo	**viajo**	Yo	**viajé**
Tú	**viajas**	Tú	**viajaste**
Él/Ella/Ud.	**viaja**	Él/Ella/Ud.	**viajó**
Nosotros	**viajamos**	Nosotros	**viajamos**
Vosotros	**viajáis**	Vosotros	**viajasteis**
Ellos/Ellas/Uds.	**viajan**	Ellos/Ellas/Uds.	**viajaron**

hablar

a-BLAR (*v.*): to speak

When the announcer *speaks* his words are <u>*a blur*</u>,
and the crowd is so loud they can't hear a word.

PRESENT TENSE		PRETERITE TENSE	
Yo	hablo	Yo	hablé
Tú	hablas	Tú	hablaste
Él/Ella/Ud.	habla	Él/Ella/Ud.	habló
Nosotros	hablamos	Nosotros	hablamos
Vosotros	habláis	Vosotros	hablasteis
Ellos/Ellas/Uds.	hablan	Ellos/Ellas/Uds.	hablaron

DRILL 4

Refresh Your Memory

Match the word and link to its corresponding definition.

1. sentarse (centaur)
2. resfriarse (rest, Friar … say)
3. casarse (cars are, says)
4. atreverse (ah, Trevor, says)
5. asustarse (sue the star, says)
6. enfadarse (fad … says)
7. reírse (rear say)
8. llegar (Hagar)
9. viajar (via jar)
10. hablar (a blur)

A. to scare
B. to marry
C. to speak
D. to catch a cold
E. to travel
F. to dare
G. to laugh
H. to sit down
I. to anger, annoy
J. to arrive

Test Your Knowledge

Fill in the blanks with the present tense of the appropriate verb, except where indicated.

1. Daniel, ¿ _____ a hacer paracaidismo?

2. Me voy a poner la bufanda. Hace mucho frío y no quiero _____.

3. Las cuatro amigas _____ [preterite] juntas en la cafetería.

4. El gato _____ [preterite] cuando ladró el perro.

5. _____ [preterite] cuando te dije que no iba a la fiesta.

6. Yo _____ por teléfono con mi madre cada domingo.

7. El niño _____ [preterite] cuando le hice cosquillas.

8. Mis padres _____ [preterite] en el 1970. Este año celebraron 37 años juntos.

9. ¿Cuándo _____ el vuelo de Quito?

10. Mi hermana y su esposo _____ a Madrid todos los años.

comprar

kom-PRAR **(v.)**: to buy, purchase

"Buy this polka-dot dress; it's outta sight!"
"You'll want to wear it <u>come prom</u> night."

PRESENT TENSE		PRETERITE TENSE	
Yo	compro	Yo	compré
Tú	compras	Tú	compraste
Él/Ella/Ud.	compra	Él/Ella/Ud.	compró
Nosotros	compramos	Nosotros	compramos
Vosotros	compráis	Vosotros	comprasteis
Ellos/Ellas/Uds.	compran	Ellos/Ellas/Uds.	compraron

ir

EER (*v.*): to go

Like Van Gogh, his *ear* had *to go*.

PRESENT TENSE		PRETERITE TENSE	
Yo	**voy**	Yo	**fui**
Tú	**vas**	Tú	**fuiste**
Él/Ella/Ud.	**va**	Él/Ella/Ud.	**fue**
Nosotros	**vamos**	Nosotros	**fuimos**
Vosotros	**vais**	Vosotros	**fuisteis**
Ellos/Ellas/Uds.	**van**	Ellos/Ellas/Uds.	**fueron**

hacer

a–SER **(v.): to do, make**

A Sir is always sure *to do*
what Queen and country tell him to.

PRESENT TENSE		PRETERITE TENSE	
Yo	hago	Yo	hice
Tú	haces	Tú	hiciste
Él/Ella/Ud.	hace	Él/Ella/Ud.	hizo
Nosotros	hacemos	Nosotros	hicimos
Vosotros	hacéis	Vosotros	hicisteis
Ellos/Ellas/Uds.	hacen	Ellos/Ellas/Uds.	hicieron

conducir

kon-doo-SEER **(v.):** to drive

The wild _conductor_ _drives_ off the rails
while the passengers inside holler, scream, and wail.

PRESENT TENSE		PRETERITE TENSE	
Yo	conduzco	Yo	conduje
Tú	conduces	Tú	condujiste
Él/Ella/Ud.	conduce	Él/Ella/Ud.	condujo
Nosotros	conducimos	Nosotros	conducimos
Vosotros	conducís	Vosotros	condujisteis
Ellos/Ellas/Uds.	conducen	Ellos/Ellas/Uds.	condujeron

conocer

ko-no-SER (*v.*): to know (person, place)

The warden *knows* burly Carl, so he won't stare
at his wild tattoos and his _con nose hair_.

PRESENT TENSE		PRETERITE TENSE	
Yo	conozco	Yo	conocí
Tú	conoces	Tú	conociste
Él/Ella/Ud.	conoce	Él/Ella/Ud.	conoció
Nosotros	conocemos	Nosotros	conocíamos
Vosotros	conocéis	Vosotros	conocisteis
Ellos/Ellas/Uds.	conocen	Ellos/Ellas/Uds.	conocieron

traducir

tra-doo-SEER (*v.*): to translate

**My new friend's from Spain, let me _introduce her_—
can you *translate* for me as I try to seduce her?**

PRESENT TENSE		PRETERITE TENSE	
Yo	traduzco	Yo	traduje
Tú	traduces	Tú	tradujiste
Él/Ella/Ud.	traduce	Él/Ella/Ud.	tradujo
Nosotros	traducimos	Nosotros	tradujimos
Vosotros	traducís	Vosotros	tradujisteis
Ellos/Ellas/Uds.	traducen	Ellos/Ellas/Uds.	tradujeron

saber

sa-BER (*v.*): to know (fact, skill)

The terrible Darth Vader
knows **how to use his** <u>saber</u>.

PRESENT TENSE		PRETERITE TENSE	
Yo	sé	Yo	supe
Tú	sabes	Tú	supiste
Él/Ella/Ud.	sabe	Él/Ella/Ud.	supo
Nosotros	sabemos	Nosotros	supimos
Vosotros	sabéis	Vosotros	supisteis
Ellos/Ellas/Uds.	saben	Ellos/Ellas/Uds.	supieron

llevar

ye-VAR (*v.*): to bring, take

Millionaire Var *brings* beer from the bar, and his thirsty friends all cry, "*Yay, Var!*"

PRESENT TENSE		PRETERITE TENSE	
Yo	llevo	Yo	llevé
Tú	llevas	Tú	llevaste
Él/Ella/Ud.	lleva	Él/Ella/Ud.	llevó
Nosotros	llevamos	Nosotros	llevamos
Vosotros	lleváis	Vosotros	llevasteis
Ellos/Ellas/Uds.	llevan	Ellos/Ellas/Uds.	llevaron

pedir

pe-DEER (*v.*): to ask

**Don't *ask* the <u>pet deer</u>
if hunting season is near.**

PRESENT TENSE		PRETERITE TENSE	
Yo	**pido**	Yo	**pedí**
Tú	**pides**	Tú	**pediste**
Él/Ella/Ud.	**pide**	Él/Ella/Ud.	**pidió**
Nosotros	**pedimos**	Nosotros	**pedimos**
Vosotros	**pedís**	Vosotros	**pedisteis**
Ellos/Ellas/Uds.	**piden**	Ellos/Ellas/Uds.	**pidieron**

preguntar

pre-goon-TAR (*v.*): to ask

**Steve *asked* a question that got him slapped,
"Are you *pregnant*, or are you fat?"**

PRESENT TENSE		PRETERITE TENSE	
Yo	**pregunto**	Yo	**pregunté**
Tú	**preguntas**	Tú	**preguntaste**
Él/Ella/Ud.	**pregunta**	Él/Ella/Ud.	**preguntó**
Nosotros	**preguntamos**	Nosotros	**preguntamos**
Vosotros	**preguntáis**	Vosotros	**preguntasteis**
Ellos/Ellas/Uds.	**preguntan**	Ellos/Ellas/Uds.	**preguntaron**

DRILL 5

Refresh Your Memory

Match the word and link to its corresponding definition.

1. comprar (come prom) B
2. ir (ear) D
3. hacer (a Sir) F
4. conducir (conductor) C
5. conocer (con nose hair) A
6. traducir (introduce her) I
7. saber (saber) H
8. llevar (yay, Var!) G
9. pedir (pet deer) E
10. preguntar (pregnant) J

A. to know (person, place)
B. to buy, purchase
C. to drive
D. to go
E. to ask for
F. to do, make
G. to bring, take
H. to know (fact, skill)
I. to translate
J. to ask

Test Your Knowledge

Fill in the blanks with the present tense of the appropriate verb, except where indicated.

1. Cuando estoy aburrida, _hago_ dibujos en mi cuaderno.

2. La semana pasada mi familia _fue_ [preterite] a un partido de fútbol.

3. A Hernán le gusta _conducir_ su carro nuevo.

4. La señora Martínez _compró_ [preterite] una caja de huevos en el supermercado.

5. La licenciada Fernandez _llevó_ [preterite] su computadora portátil en el viaje.

6. El traductor _tradujo_ [preterite] el guión de inglés a español.

7. Catalina _sabe_ hablar tres idiomas: español, francés, e italiano.

8. Te _pido_ que no le digas nada a mi madre.

9. Vosotras me _preguntasteis_ [preterite] si había hecho la tarea.

10. Juan Carlos, ¿ _conoce_ a mi hermana, Claudia?

jugar

hoo-GAR (*v.*): to play (a sport)

Who guards our goal from the other team?
When hairy Gary the goalie *plays*, opponents scream.

PRESENT TENSE		PRETERITE TENSE	
Yo	juego	Yo	jugué
Tú	juegas	Tú	jugaste
Él/Ella/Ud.	juega	Él/Ella/Ud.	jugó
Nosotros	jugamos	Nosotros	jugamos
Vosotros	jugáis	Vosotros	jugasteis
Ellos/Ellas/Uds.	juegan	Ellos/Ellas/Uds.	jugaron

tocar

to-KAR (*v.*): to play (an instrument)

We *took our* instruments and loudly *played*
as we marched down the road in the small-town parade.

PRESENT TENSE		PRETERITE TENSE	
Yo	toco	Yo	toqué
Tú	tocas	Tú	tocaste
Él/Ella/Ud.	toca	Él/Ella/Ud.	tocó
Nosotros	tocamos	Nosotros	tocamos
Vosotros	tocáis	Vosotros	tocasteis
Ellos/Ellas/Uds.	tocan	Ellos/Ellas/Uds.	tocaron

sacar

sa-KAR (*v.*): to take

Sal's old, broken-down *car*
won't *take* him out very far.

PRESENT TENSE		PRETERITE TENSE	
Yo	saco	Yo	saqué
Tú	sacas	Tú	sacaste
Él/Ella/Ud.	saca	Él/Ella/Ud.	sacó
Nosotros	sacamos	Nosotros	sacamos
Vosotros	sacáis	Vosotros	sacasteis
Ellos/Ellas/Uds.	sacan	Ellos/Ellas/Uds.	sacaron

empezar

em-pe-SAR (*v.*): to begin

**The chubby _emperor_ begins
his restrictive diet to get strong and thin.**

PRESENT TENSE		PRETERITE TENSE	
Yo	empiezo	Yo	empecé
Tú	empiezas	Tú	empezaste
Él/Ella/Ud.	empieza	Él/Ella/Ud.	empezó
Nosotros	empezamos	Nosotros	empezamos
Vosotros	empezáis	Vosotros	empezasteis
Ellos/Ellas/Uds.	empiezan	Ellos/Ellas/Uds.	empezaron

romperse

rom-PER-se (*v.*): to break

The <u>rompers say</u> that they will get their way,
or they'll *break* your toys and ruin your day.

<table>
<tr><td colspan="2">PRESENT TENSE</td><td colspan="2">PRETERITE TENSE</td></tr>
<tr><td align="right">Yo</td><td>me rompo</td><td align="right">Yo</td><td>me rompí</td></tr>
<tr><td align="right">Tú</td><td>te rompes</td><td align="right">Tú</td><td>te rompiste</td></tr>
<tr><td align="right">Él/Ella/Ud.</td><td>se rompe</td><td align="right">Él/Ella/Ud.</td><td>se rompió</td></tr>
<tr><td align="right">Nosotros</td><td>nos rompemos</td><td align="right">Nosotros</td><td>nos rompimos</td></tr>
<tr><td align="right">Vosotros</td><td>os rompéis</td><td align="right">Vosotros</td><td>os rompisteis</td></tr>
<tr><td align="right">Ellos/Ellas/Uds.</td><td>se rompen</td><td align="right">Ellos/Ellas/Uds.</td><td>se rompieron</td></tr>
</table>

regar

re-GAR (*v.*): to water

The gardener forgot *to water* his plot,
so now he'll have to _re-garden_ that spot.

PRESENT TENSE		PRETERITE TENSE	
Yo	riego	Yo	regué
Tú	riegas	Tú	regaste
Él/Ella/Ud.	riega	Él/Ella/Ud.	regó
Nosotros	regamos	Nosotros	regamos
Vosotros	regáis	Vosotros	regasteis
Ellos/Ellas/Uds.	riegan	Ellos/Ellas/Uds.	regaron

tener

te-NER (*v.*): to have

The babysitter thinks a _tenner_ is fair for each hour she'll *have* the child in her care.

PRESENT TENSE		PRETERITE TENSE	
Yo	tengo	Yo	tuve
Tú	tienes	Tú	tuviste
Él/Ella/Ud.	tiene	Él/Ella/Ud.	tuvo
Nosotros	tenemos	Nosotros	tuvimos
Vosotros	tenéis	Vosotros	tuvisteis
Ellos/Ellas/Uds.	tienen	Ellos/Ellas/Uds.	tuvieron

venir

ve-NEER (*v.*): to come

Hey muscle man, did you park this _van here_?
Come **over and help us pack up our gear.**

PRESENT TENSE		PRETERITE TENSE	
Yo	**vengo**	Yo	**vine**
Tú	**vienes**	Tú	**viniste**
Él/Ella/Ud.	**viene**	Él/Ella/Ud.	**vino**
Nosotros	**venimos**	Nosotros	**vinimos**
Vosotros	**venís**	Vosotros	**vinisteis**
Ellos/Ellas/Uds.	**vienen**	Ellos/Ellas/Uds.	**vinieron**

ver

ver **(*v.*): to see**

The conductor told his orchestra to rehearse the _verse_ and *to see* each note as a melodious burst.

PRESENT TENSE		PRETERITE TENSE	
Yo	**veo**	Yo	**vi**
Tú	**ves**	Tú	**viste**
Él/Ella/Ud.	**ve**	Él/Ella/Ud.	**vio**
Nosotros	**vemos**	Nosotros	**vimos**
Vosotros	**véis**	Vosotros	**visteis**
Ellos/Ellas/Uds.	**ven**	Ellos/Ellas/Uds.	**vieron**

correr

ko-RER (*v.*): to run

The orange said, "No more
will I *run* with the apple <u>core</u>."

PRESENT TENSE		PRETERITE TENSE	
Yo	corro	Yo	corrí
Tú	corres	Tú	corriste
Él/Ella/Ud.	corre	Él/Ella/Ud.	corrió
Nosotros	corremos	Nosotros	corrimos
Vosotros	corréis	Vosotros	corristeis
Ellos/Ellas/Uds.	corren	Ellos/Ellas/Uds.	corrieron

DRILL 6

Refresh Your Memory

Match the word and link to its corresponding definition.

1. jugar (who guards)
2. tocar (took our)
3. sacar (Sal's ... car)
4. empezar (emperor)
5. romperse (rompers say)
6. regar (re-garden)
7. tener (tenner)
8. venir (van here)
9. ver (verse)
10. correr (core)

A. to play (an instrument)
B. to break
C. to play (a sport)
D. to have
E. to begin
F. to come
G. to water
H. to run
I. to take
J. to see

Test Your Knowledge

Fill in the blanks with the present tense of the appropriate verb, except where indicated.

1. Todas las mañanas _____ en la pista del gimnasio.

2. ¿Cual instrumento _____, Carlos?

3. La película _____ [preterite] a las tres en punto.

4. El niño _____ [preterite] el florero de cerámica.

5. Durante nuestra vacación en México, _____ [preterite] muchas fotografías.

6. Rosa y Carlos, ¿ _____ a la fiesta con nosotros?

7. ¿Te olvidaste de _____ las plantas? Están secas.

8. Mi abuela _____ [preterite] cirugía cardíaca el año pasado.

9. Papá, ¿ _____ [preterite] el avión que acaba de pasar?

10. Los niños _____ con la pelota en el plaza.

cerrar

e-RAR (*v.*): to close

Close the cellar door,
or else hear *Sarah* snore.

PRESENT TENSE		PRETERITE TENSE	
Yo	**cierro**	Yo	**cerré**
Tú	**cierras**	Tú	**cerraste**
Él/Ella/Ud.	**cierra**	Él/Ella/Ud.	**cerró**
Nosotros	**cerramos**	Nosotros	**cerramos**
Vosotros	**cerráis**	Vosotros	**cerrasteis**
Ellos/Ellas/Uds.	**cierran**	Ellos/Ellas/Uds.	**cierran**

ganar

ga-NAR (*v.*): to win

Coach says time's getting thin:
We must *gain our* courage *to win*.

PRESENT TENSE		PRETERITE TENSE	
Yo	gano	Yo	gané
Tú	ganas	Tú	ganaste
Él/Ella/Ud.	gana	Él/Ella/Ud.	ganó
Nosotros	ganamos	Nosotros	ganamos
Vosotros	ganáis	Vosotros	ganasteis
Ellos/Ellas/Uds.	ganan	Ellos/Ellas/Uds.	ganaron

compartir

kom-par-TEER (*v.*): to share

Come party with the drunken flies.
They'll *share* the crumbs from cakes and pies.

PRESENT TENSE		PRETERITE TENSE	
Yo	comparto	Yo	compartí
Tú	compartes	Tú	compartiste
Él/Ella/Ud.	comparte	Él/Ella/Ud.	compartió
Nosotros	compartimos	Nosotros	compartimos
Vosotros	compartís	Vosotros	compartisteis
Ellos/Ellas/Uds.	comparten	Ellos/Ellas/Uds.	compartieron

enseñar

en-se-NYAR **(v.)**: to teach

Come hear what teachers fear:
It's tough *to teach* *in senior year*.

PRESENT TENSE		PRETERITE TENSE	
Yo	enseño	Yo	enseñé
Tú	enseñas	Tú	enseñaste
Él/Ella/Ud.	enseña	Él/Ella/Ud.	enseñó
Nosotros	enseñamos	Nosotros	enseñamos
Vosotros	enseñáis	Vosotros	enseñasteis
Ellos/Ellas/Uds.	enseñan	Ellos/Ellas/Uds.	enseñaron

gustar

goo-STAR (*v.*): to like

**A naughty little _gust of air_
likes messing up the lady's hair.**

PRESENT TENSE		PRETERITE TENSE	
Yo	**gusto**	Yo	**gusté**
Tú	**gustas**	Tú	**gustaste**
Él/Ella/Ud.	**gusta**	Él/Ella/Ud.	**gustó**
Nosotros	**gustamos**	Nosotros	**gustamos**
Vosotros	**gustáis**	Vosotros	**gustasteis**
Ellos/Ellas/Uds.	**gustan**	Ellos/Ellas/Uds.	**gustaron**

perder

per-DER (*v.*): to lose, miss (the train)

Frightened Claire *loses* a dollar *per dare*:
She can't bear to be scared and must give up her fare.

PRESENT TENSE		PRETERITE TENSE	
Yo	**pierdo**	Yo	**perdí**
Tú	**pierdes**	Tú	**perdiste**
Él/Ella/Ud.	**pierde**	Él/Ella/Ud.	**perdió**
Nosotros	**perdemos**	Nosotros	**perdimos**
Vosotros	**perdéis**	Vosotros	**perdisteis**
Ellos/Ellas/Uds.	**pierden**	Ellos/Ellas/Uds.	**perdieron**

llorar

yo-RAR (*v.*): to cry

**Said the mouse to the lion with a tiny sigh,
"I promise if _you roar_, I'll _cry_!"**

PRESENT TENSE		PRETERITE TENSE	
Yo	**lloro**	Yo	**lloré**
Tú	**lloras**	Tú	**lloraste**
Él/Ella/Ud.	**llora**	Él/Ella/Ud.	**lloró**
Nosotros	**lloramos**	Nosotros	**lloramos**
Vosotros	**lloráis**	Vosotros	**llorasteis**
Ellos/Ellas/Uds.	**lloran**	Ellos/Ellas/Uds.	**lloraron**

volver

vol-VER **(v.):** to return (to a place)

**After completing its terrible chore,
the cob of corn *returned* the <u>*revolver*</u> to the drawer.**

PRESENT TENSE		PRETERITE TENSE	
Yo	**vuelvo**	Yo	**volví**
Tú	**vuelves**	Tú	**volviste**
Él/Ella/Ud.	**vuelve**	Él/Ella/Ud.	**volvió**
Nosotros	**volvemos**	Nosotros	**volvimos**
Vosotros	**volvéis**	Vosotros	**volvisteis**
Ellos/Ellas/Uds.	**vuelven**	Ellos/Ellas/Uds.	**volvieron**

olvidar

ol-vee-DAR (*v.*): to forget

**Forgetful Frankie can't see very far—
he *forgot* his glass eye in the *olive jar*.**

PRESENT TENSE		PRETERITE TENSE	
Yo	olvido	Yo	olvidé
Tú	olvidas	Tú	olvidaste
Él/Ella/Ud.	olvida	Él/Ella/Ud.	olvidó
Nosotros	olvidamos	Nosotros	olvidamos
Vosotros	olvidáis	Vosotros	olvidasteis
Ellos/Ellas/Uds.	olvidan	Ellos/Ellas/Uds.	olvidaron

escoger

e–sko–HER (*v.*): to choose

Ask her to choose and you'll probably snooze:
Sue's so indecisive, she can never pick shoes.

PRESENT TENSE		PRETERITE TENSE	
Yo	escojo	Yo	escogí
Tú	escoges	Tú	escogiste
Él/Ella/Ud.	escoge	Él/Ella/Ud.	escogió
Nosotros	escogemos	Nosotros	escogimos
Vosotros	escogéis	Vosotros	escogisteis
Ellos/Ellas/Uds.	escogen	Ellos/Ellas/Uds.	escogieron

DRILL 7

Refresh Your Memory

Match the word and link to its corresponding definition.

1. cerrar (Sarah)
2. ganar (gain our)
3. compartir (come party)
4. enseñar (in senior year)
5. gustar (gust of air)
6. perder (per dare)
7. llorar (you roar)
8. volver (revolver)
9. olvidar (olive jar)
10. escoger (ask her)

A. to cry
B. to like
C. to share
D. to return (to a place)
E. to close
F. to choose
G. to win
H. to forget
I. to teach
J. to lose, miss (the train)

Test Your Knowledge

Fill in the blanks with the present tense of the appropriate verb, except where indicated.

1. Nosotros _____ [preterite] una licuadora en la rifa.

2. Después de muchos años en exilio, el escritor _____ [preterite] a su patria.

3. ¿Cuál de los dos postres vas a _____? ¿El flan o el helado?

4. Mi abuela nos _____ [preterite] como hacer tortillas de maíz.

5. ¿Quieres _____ el bocadillo conmigo? No lo puedo comer sola.

6. A los niños generalmente les _____ los caramelos.

7. Estoy tarde porque _____ [preterite] el bus.

8. Apúrate: el restaurante _____ a medianoche.

9. El bebé hambriento _____ [preterite] toda la noche.

10. Mi mamá siempre _____ mi número de teléfono.

poder

po-DER (*v.*): to be able to

**Edgar Allan *Poe dares* the maiden
to be able to befriend a raven.**

PRESENT TENSE		PRETERITE TENSE	
Yo	**puedo**	Yo	**pude**
Tú	**puedes**	Tú	**pudiste**
Él/Ella/Ud.	**puede**	Él/Ella/Ud.	**pudo**
Nosotros	**podemos**	Nosotros	**pudimos**
Vosotros	**podéis**	Vosotros	**pudisteis**
Ellos/Ellas/Uds.	**pueden**	Ellos/Ellas/Uds.	**pudieron**

asistir

a-see-STEER (*v.*): to attend

At sea, steer with a rudder and sails.
Attend to the wind, or go overboard and be lunch for the whale.

PRESENT TENSE		PRETERITE TENSE	
Yo	asisto	Yo	asistí
Tú	asistes	Tú	asististe
Él/Ella/Ud.	asiste	Él/Ella/Ud.	asistió
Nosotros	asistimos	Nosotros	asistimos
Vosotros	asistís	Vosotros	asististeis
Ellos/Ellas/Uds.	asisten	Ellos/Ellas/Uds.	asistieron

dormir

dor-MEER (*v.*): to sleep

Instead of a bed, Jake *sleeps* on a <u>door here</u>,
so every morning he awakes with a sore ear.

PRESENT TENSE		PRETERITE TENSE	
Yo	**duermo**	Yo	**dormí**
Tú	**duermes**	Tú	**dormiste**
Él/Ella/Ud.	**duerme**	Él/Ella/Ud.	**durmió**
Nosotros	**dormimos**	Nosotros	**dormimos**
Vosotros	**dormís**	Vosotros	**dormisteis**
Ellos/Ellas/Uds.	**duermen**	Ellos/Ellas/Uds.	**durmieron**

cantar

kan-TAR (*v.*): to sing

The audience *can't argue* with the opera's bad reviews:
When the soprano *sings*, it gives them all the blues.

PRESENT TENSE		PRETERITE TENSE	
Yo	canto	Yo	canté
Tú	cantas	Tú	cantaste
Él/Ella/Ud.	canta	Él/Ella/Ud.	cantó
Nosotros	cantamos	Nosotros	cantamos
Vosotros	cantáis	Vosotros	cantasteis
Ellos/Ellas/Uds.	cantan	Ellos/Ellas/Uds.	cantaron

odiar

o-dee-AR (*v.*): to hate

"*Oh dear!*" says the stodgy adult. "It's not nice *to hate*.
You really should try to get along with your mate."

PRESENT TENSE		PRETERITE TENSE	
Yo	odio	Yo	odié
Tú	odias	Tú	odiaste
Él/Ella/Ud.	odia	Él/Ella/Ud.	odió
Nosotros	odiamos	Nosotros	odiamos
Vosotros	odiáis	Vosotros	odiasteis
Ellos/Ellas/Uds.	odian	Ellos/Ellas/Uds.	odiaron

contar

kon-TAR (*v.*): to tell [a story]

Jake was <u>con</u>stantly <u>tar</u>dy, and his teacher grew irate;
he was always *telling stories* to explain why
he was late.

PRESENT TENSE		PRETERITE TENSE	
Yo	cuento	Yo	conté
Tú	cuentas	Tú	contaste
Él/Ella/Ud.	cuenta	Él/Ella/Ud.	contó
Nosotros	contamos	Nosotros	contamos
Vosotros	contáis	Vosotros	contasteis
Ellos/Ellas/Uds.	cuentan	Ellos/Ellas/Uds.	contaron

querer

ke-RER (*v.*): to want, wish

**Denise most desperately *wishes*
to have a *career* scuba-diving with fishes.**

PRESENT TENSE		PRETERITE TENSE	
Yo	quiero	Yo	quise
Tú	quieres	Tú	quisiste
Él/Ella/Ud.	quiere	Él/Ella/Ud.	quiso
Nosotros	queremos	Nosotros	quisimos
Vosotros	queréis	Vosotros	quisisteis
Ellos/Ellas/Uds.	quieren	Ellos/Ellas/Uds.	quisieron

mostrar

mo-STRAR (*v.*): to show

The _monster_ showed us his claws,
as well as his giant and powerful jaws.

PRESENT TENSE		PRETERITE TENSE	
Yo	**muestro**	Yo	**mostré**
Tú	**muestras**	Tú	**mostraste**
Él/Ella/Ud.	**muestra**	Él/Ella/Ud.	**mostró**
Nosotros	**mostramos**	Nosotros	**mostramos**
Vosotros	**mostráis**	Vosotros	**mostrasteis**
Ellos/Ellas/Uds.	**muestran**	Ellos/Ellas/Uds.	**mostraron**

recordar

re-kor-DAR (*v.*): to remember, remind

First he took out a gun and held up the store. Then he stole a car...

The reporter used a tape *recorder* to remember his story in the proper order.

PRESENT TENSE		PRETERITE TENSE	
Yo	**recuerdo**	Yo	**recordé**
Tú	**recuerdas**	Tú	**recordaste**
Él/Ella/Ud.	**recuerda**	Él/Ella/Ud.	**recordó**
Nosotros	**recordamos**	Nosotros	**recordamos**
Vosotros	**recordáis**	Vosotros	**recordasteis**
Ellos/Ellas/Uds.	**recuerdan**	Ellos/Ellas/Uds.	**recordaron**

amar

a–MAR (*v.*): to love

The girlfriend said her *love* could never be <u>marred</u>,
unless, of course, he refused her his bank card.

PRESENT TENSE		PRETERITE TENSE	
Yo	amo	Yo	amé
Tú	amas	Tú	amaste
Él/Ella/Ud.	ama	Él/Ella/Ud.	amó
Nosotros	amamos	Nosotros	amamos
Vosotros	amáis	Vosotros	amasteis
Ellos/Ellas/Uds.	aman	Ellos/Ellas/Uds.	amaron

DRILL 8

Refresh Your Memory

Match the word and link to its corresponding definition.

1. poder (Poe dares)
2. asistir (at sea, steer)
3. dormir (door here)
4. cantar (can't argue)
5. odiar (oh dear!)
6. contar (constantly tardy)
7. querer (career)
8. mostrar (monster)
9. recordar (recorder)
10. amar (marred)

A. to tell (a story)
B. to sing
C. to show
D. to hate
E. to love
F. to sleep
G. to remember
H. to want, wish
I. to be able to
J. to attend

Test Your Knowledge

Fill in the blanks with the present tense of the appropriate verb, except where indicated.

1. Juan Pablo _____ [preterite] a una universidad muy prestigiosa.
2. Es difícil, pero sé que _____ hacerlo.
3. Al final del concierto, el coro _____ [preterite] Ave María.
4. Anoche yo no _____ [preterite] bien. Tuve pesadillas.
5. No me gustan las zanahorias: de hecho, las _____.
6. El doctor Cuevas siempre _____ [preterite] ser médico.
7. Abuelita, ¿me _____ la historia de nuevo?
8. Alejandro, me _____ [preterite] su mochila nueva.
9. Los novios se _____ mucho y piensan casarse.
10. ¿Te _____ de mí? Estudiamos juntas en la universidad.

montar

mon-TAR (*v.*): to climb, go up

As we *climbed* the <u>mount, our</u> legs began to lift;
we wished we had a ride—that would be a gift!

PRESENT TENSE		PRETERITE TENSE	
Yo	monto	Yo	monté
Tú	montas	Tú	montaste
Él/Ella/Ud.	monta	Él/Ella/Ud.	montó
Nosotros	montamos	Nosotros	montamos
Vosotros	montáis	Vosotros	montasteis
Ellos/Ellas/Uds.	montan	Ellos/Ellas/Uds.	montaron

escuchar

e–skoo–CHAR (*v.*): to listen

The design students *listened* but rolled their eyes,
as they discussed Miss *Essie's cool chair* made of flies.

PRESENT TENSE		PRETERITE TENSE	
Yo	escucho	Yo	escuché
Tú	escuchas	Tú	escuchaste
Él/Ella/Ud.	escucha	Él/Ella/Ud.	escuchó
Nosotros	escuchamos	Nosotros	escuchamos
Vosotros	escucháis	Vosotros	escuchasteis
Ellos/Ellas/Uds.	escuchan	Ellos/Ellas/Uds.	escucharon

sonreír

son-re-EER (*v.*): to smile

**Chelsea's so friendly and filled with good cheer;
when she *smiles* it's like the <u>sun ear-to-ear</u>.**

PRESENT TENSE		PRETERITE TENSE	
Yo	sonrío	Yo	sonreí
Tú	sonríes	Tú	sonreíste
Él/Ella/Ud.	sonríe	Él/Ella/Ud.	sonrió
Nosotros	sonreímos	Nosotros	sonreímos
Vosotros	sonreís	Vosotros	sonreísteis
Ellos/Ellas/Uds.	sonríen	Ellos/Ellas/Uds.	sonrieron

vestirse

ve-STEER-se (*v.*): to get dressed

**On their hangers were his shorts and his _vest_,
but without his _spear_, the warrior couldn't _get dressed_.**

PRESENT TENSE		PRETERITE TENSE	
Yo	me visto	Yo	me vestí
Tú	te vistes	Tú	te vestiste
Él/Ella/Ud.	se viste	Él/Ella/Ud.	se vistió
Nosotros	nos vestimos	Nosotros	nos vestimos
Vosotros	os vestís	Vosotros	os vestisteis
Ellos/Ellas/Uds.	se visten	Ellos/Ellas/Uds.	se vistieron

subir

soo-BEER **(v.)**: to go up, climb, raise

"Can a person _sue beer_?" asked old drunken Will.
"If it weren't for beer, I'd never have _climbed_ this hill."

PRESENT TENSE		PRETERITE TENSE	
Yo	**subo**	Yo	**subí**
Tú	**subes**	Tú	**subiste**
Él/Ella/Ud.	**sube**	Él/Ella/Ud.	**subió**
Nosotros	**subimos**	Nosotros	**subimos**
Vosotros	**subís**	Vosotros	**subisteis**
Ellos/Ellas/Uds.	**suben**	Ellos/Ellas/Uds.	**subieron**

contestar

kon-te-STAR (*v.*): to answer

"Let's watch that _contest_ with ants.
The one who *answers* gets six-legged pants."

PRESENT TENSE		PRETERITE TENSE	
Yo	contesto	Yo	contesté
Tú	contestas	Tú	contestaste
Él/Ella/Ud.	contesta	Él/Ella/Ud.	contestó
Nosotros	contestamos	Nosotros	contestamos
Vosotros	contestáis	Vosotros	contestasteis
Ellos/Ellas/Uds.	contestan	Ellos/Ellas/Uds.	contestaron

barrer

ba-RER (*v.*): to sweep

**The old _bar_ next door has a _rare_ piece of lore:
For good luck inside, they don't _sweep_ the floor.**

PRESENT TENSE		PRETERITE TENSE	
Yo	barro	Yo	barrí
Tú	barres	Tú	barriste
Él/Ella/Ud.	barre	Él/Ella/Ud.	barrió
Nosotros	barremos	Nosotros	barrimos
Vosotros	barréis	Vosotros	barristeis
Ellos/Ellas/Uds.	barren	Ellos/Ellas/Uds.	barrieron

sorprender

sor-pren-DER (*v.*): to surprise, astonish

The *sorority pretended* to be *surprised* with first prize—
their superiority wasn't something they could disguise.

PRESENT TENSE		PRETERITE TENSE	
Yo	sorprendo	Yo	sorprendí
Tú	sorprendes	Tú	sorprendiste
Él/Ella/Ud.	sorprende	Él/Ella/Ud.	sorprendió
Nosotros	sorprendemos	Nosotros	sorprendimos
Vosotros	sorprendéis	Vosotros	sorprendisteis
Ellos/Ellas/Uds.	sorprenden	Ellos/Ellas/Uds.	sorprendieron

soñar

so-NYAR (*v.*): to dream

Sonia *dreamed* she was a dolphin:
She used <u>sonar</u> and swam with strong fins.

PRESENT TENSE		PRETERITE TENSE	
Yo	sueño	Yo	soñé
Tú	sueñas	Tú	soñaste
Él/Ella/Ud.	sueña	Él/Ella/Ud.	soñó
Nosotros	soñamos	Nosotros	soñamos
Vosotros	soñáis	Vosotros	soñasteis
Ellos/Ellas/Uds.	sueñan	Ellos/Ellas/Uds.	soñaron

beber

be-BER (*v.*): to drink

**Give a *baby* the wrong milk *to drink*,
and it will create a terrible stink.**

PRESENT TENSE		PRETERITE TENSE	
Yo	**bebo**	Yo	**bebí**
Tú	**bebes**	Tú	**bebiste**
Él/Ella/Ud.	**bebe**	Él/Ella/Ud.	**bebió**
Nosotros	**bebemos**	Nosotros	**bebimos**
Vosotros	**bebéis**	Vosotros	**bebisteis**
Ellos/Ellas/Uds.	**beben**	Ellos/Ellas/Uds.	**bebieron**

DRILL 9

Refresh Your Memory

Match the word and link to its corresponding definition.

1. montar (mount, our)
2. escuchar (Essie's cool chair)
3. sonreír (sun ear-to-ear)
4. vestirse (vest … spear)
5. subir (sue beer)
6. contester (contest)
7. barrer (bar … rare)
8. sorprender (sorority pretended)
9. soñar (sonar)
10. beber (baby)

A. to sweep
B. to listen
C. to answer
D. to dream
E. to climb, go up
F. to drink
G. to smile
H. to go up, climb, raise
I. to surprise, astonish
J. to get dressed

Test Your Knowledge

Fill in the blanks with the present tense of the appropriate verb, except where indicated.

1. Las hijas de la Señora Capelo _____ a caballo todos los sábados.

2. La niña _____ [preterite] cuando Javier le dio el caramelo.

3. Marta, ¿ _____ [preterite] lo que acabo de decir? ¡Apaga el televisor!

4. La viuda _____ [preterite] de negro.

5. Está sonando el teléfono: lo voy a _____.

6. El gerente le espera arriba: tiene que _____ al séptimo piso.

7. El empleado _____ el piso todos los días.

8. Anoche yo _____ [preterite] que era el rey de España.

9. Nosotros _____ [preterite] a Alicia con una fiesta sorpresa.

10. Tengo tanta sed: tenéis algo de _____?

seguir

se-GEER (*v.*): to follow

Stan *followed* Dan hiking, as he had the _set gear_,
but Dan sure didn't know how to encounter a deer.

PRESENT TENSE		PRETERITE TENSE	
Yo	sigo	Yo	seguí
Tú	sigues	Tú	seguiste
Él/Ella/Ud.	sigue	Él/Ella/Ud.	siguió
Nosotros	seguimos	Nosotros	seguimos
Vosotros	seguís	Vosotros	seguisteis
Ellos/Ellas/Uds.	siguen	Ellos/Ellas/Uds.	siguieron

saltar

sal-TAR (*v.*): to jump, leap, spring

**We gardeners always <u>salt our</u> slugs,
or they'll *leap* through our flowers and slime the bugs.**

PRESENT TENSE		PRETERITE TENSE	
Yo	**salto**	Yo	**salté**
Tú	**saltas**	Tú	**saltaste**
Él/Ella/Ud.	**salta**	Él/Ella/Ud.	**saltó**
Nosotros	**saltamos**	Nosotros	**saltamos**
Vosotros	**saltáis**	Vosotros	**saltasteis**
Ellos/Ellas/Uds.	**saltan**	Ellos/Ellas/Uds.	**saltaron**

tirar

tee-RAR (*v.*): to throw away

The *tearful artist threw away* his art and started to sob when he heard the comments of the critiquing mob.

PRESENT TENSE		PRETERITE TENSE	
Yo	tiro	Yo	tiré
Tú	tiras	Tú	tiraste
Él/Ella/Ud.	tira	Él/Ella/Ud.	tiró
Nosotros	tiramos	Nosotros	tiramos
Vosotros	tiráis	Vosotros	tirasteis
Ellos/Ellas/Uds.	tiran	Ellos/Ellas/Uds.	tiraron

besar

be-SAR (*v.*): to kiss

Ben knew he'd <u>*be sorry*</u> to miss her,
which is why he skipped class and tried *to kiss* her.

PRESENT TENSE		PRETERITE TENSE	
Yo	**beso**	Yo	**besé**
Tú	**besas**	Tú	**besaste**
Él/Ella/Ud.	**besa**	Él/Ella/Ud.	**besó**
Nosotros	**besamos**	Nosotros	**besamos**
Vosotros	**besáis**	Vosotros	**besasteis**
Ellos/Ellas/Uds.	**besan**	Ellos/Ellas/Uds.	**besaron**

deber

de-BER (*v.*): to owe, must, should

Unless she wants to share,
Hanna *must* hide her food from *the bear*.

PRESENT TENSE		PRETERITE TENSE	
Yo	debo	Yo	debí
Tú	debes	Tú	debiste
Él/Ella/Ud.	debe	Él/Ella/Ud.	debió
Nosotros	debemos	Nosotros	debimos
Vosotros	debéis	Vosotros	debisteis
Ellos/Ellas/Uds.	deben	Ellos/Ellas/Uds.	debieron

pintar

peen-TAR (*v.*): to paint

The friends *pinned a tiara* to the bachelorette's head,
then they all set out *to paint* the town red.

PRESENT TENSE		PRETERITE TENSE	
Yo	pinto	Yo	pinté
Tú	pintas	Tú	pintaste
Él/Ella/Ud.	pinta	Él/Ella/Ud.	pintó
Nosotros	pintamos	Nosotros	pintamos
Vosotros	pintáis	Vosotros	pintasteis
Ellos/Ellas/Uds.	pintan	Ellos/Ellas/Uds.	pintaron

descubrir

de-skoo-BREER (*v.*): to discover

Behind the school, Doug *discovered* the _desk o' beer_;
a drunken leprechaun must have left it here.

PRESENT TENSE		PRETERITE TENSE	
Yo	descubro	Yo	descubrí
Tú	descubres	Tú	descubriste
Él/Ella/Ud.	descubre	Él/Ella/Ud.	descubrió
Nosotros	descubrimos	Nosotros	descubrimos
Vosotros	descubrís	Vosotros	descubristeis
Ellos/Ellas/Uds.	descubren	Ellos/Ellas/Uds.	descubrieron

cortar

kor-TAR (*v.*): to cut

In *court, our* case was *cut* short
when the lawyer sneezed on a crucial report.

PRESENT TENSE		PRETERITE TENSE	
Yo	**corto**	Yo	**corté**
Tú	**cortas**	Tú	**cortaste**
Él/Ella/Ud.	**corta**	Él/Ella/Ud.	**cortó**
Nosotros	**cortamos**	Nosotros	**cortamos**
Vosotros	**cortáis**	Vosotros	**cortasteis**
Ellos/Ellas/Uds.	**cortan**	Ellos/Ellas/Uds.	**cortaron**

prometer

pro-me-TER (*v.*): to promise

Pam was a _pro_ at the 100 _meter_ run;
she _promised_ her teammates it was a race easily won.

PRESENT TENSE		PRETERITE TENSE	
Yo	**prometo**	Yo	**prometí**
Tú	**prometes**	Tú	**prometiste**
Él/Ella/Ud.	**promete**	Él/Ella/Ud.	**prometió**
Nosotros	**prometemos**	Nosotros	**prometimos**
Vosotros	**prometéis**	Vosotros	**prometisteis**
Ellos/Ellas/Uds.	**prometen**	Ellos/Ellas/Uds.	**prometieron**

crecer

kre-SER (*v.*): to grow

Dale tried *to grow* a beard, but the hair was too thin;
he had just a _crescent_ of fuzz on his chin.

PRESENT TENSE	
Yo	crezco
Tú	creces
Él/Ella/Ud.	crece
Nosotros	crecemos
Vosotros	crecéis
Ellos/Ellas/Uds.	crecen

PRETERITE TENSE	
Yo	crecí
Tú	creciste
Él/Ella/Ud.	creció
Nosotros	crecimos
Vosotros	crecisteis
Ellos/Ellas/Uds.	crecieron

DRILL 10

Refresh Your Memory

Match the word and link to its corresponding definition.

1. seguir (set gear)
2. saltar (salt our)
3. tirar (tearful artist)
4. besar (be sorry)
5. deber (the bear)
6. pintar (pinned a tiara)
7. descubrir (desk o' beer)
8. cortar (court, our)
9. prometer (pro ... meter)
10. crecer (crescent)

A. to jump, leap, spring
B. to paint
C. to cut
D. to follow
E. to grow
F. to throw away
G. to promise
H. to owe, must, should
I. to kiss
J. to discover

Test Your Knowledge

Fill in the blanks with the present tense of the appropriate verb, except where indicated.

1. El chico _____ [preterite] del muro y se rompió la pierna.

2. No soy capaz de _____ el argumento: es demasiado complicado.

3. Tu abuela te _____ [preterite] en amba mejilla.

4. Cuando era pequeña, yo _____ [preterite] la comida que yo no quería.

5. Diego Velásquez _____ [preterite] el cuadro Las Meninas.

6. Jorge me _____ cien pesos porque perdió la apuesta.

7. Cuando exploramos el ático de mis abuelos, _____ [preterite] un viejo álbum de fotografías.

8. Una planta no puede _____ sin luz y agua.

9. María, te _____ que nunca te traicionaré.

10. Juanito, te toca a ti _____ el césped.

preocuparse

pre-o-koo-PAR-se **(v.): to worry**

Preoccupied with *worry*, Amanda was a nail-biter.
Then she took up yoga, and her days got brighter.

PRESENT TENSE		PRETERITE TENSE	
Yo	me preocupo	Yo	me preocupé
Tú	te preocupas	Tú	te preocupaste
Él/Ella/Ud.	se preocupa	Él/Ella/Ud.	se preocupó
Nosotros	nos preocupamos	Nosotros	nos preocupamos
Vosotros	os preocupáis	Vosotros	os preocupasteis
Ellos/Ellas/Uds.	se preocupan	Ellos/Ellas/Uds.	se preocuparon

divertirse

dee-ver-TEER-se **(v.)**: to amuse, to distract
(to have a good time)

The family sought a _diversion_ from its boring routine:
They would _have a good time_ making a scene.

PRESENT TENSE		PRETERITE TENSE	
Yo	**me divierto**	Yo	**me divertí**
Tú	**te diviertes**	Tú	**te divertiste**
Él/Ella/Ud.	**se divierte**	Él/Ella/Ud.	**se divirtió**
Nosotros	**nos divertimos**	Nosotros	**nos divertimos**
Vosotros	**os divertís**	Vosotros	**os divertisteis**
Ellos/Ellas/Uds.	**se divierten**	Ellos/Ellas/Uds.	**se divirtieron**

coser

ko-SER (*v.*): to sew

**Red Riding Hood sat _closer_ to learn how *to sew*—
the wolf would show her what she needed to know.**

PRESENT TENSE		PRETERITE TENSE	
Yo	**coso**	Yo	**cosí**
Tú	**coses**	Tú	**cosiste**
Él/Ella/Ud.	**cose**	Él/Ella/Ud.	**cosió**
Nosotros	**cosemos**	Nosotros	**cosimos**
Vosotros	**coséis**	Vosotros	**cosisteis**
Ellos/Ellas/Uds.	**cosen**	Ellos/Ellas/Uds.	**cosieron**

oler

o–LER (*v.*): to smell

**The Spanish dancer danced, the crowd yelled, "*Olé!*"
but then they *smelled* his armpits and left for the day.**

PRESENT TENSE		PRETERITE TENSE	
Yo	**huelo**	Yo	**olí**
Tú	**hueles**	Tú	**oliste**
Él/Ella/Ud.	**huele**	Él/Ella/Ud.	**olió**
Nosotros	**olemos**	Nosotros	**olimos**
Vosotros	**oléis**	Vosotros	**olisteis**
Ellos/Ellas/Uds.	**huelen**	Ellos/Ellas/Uds.	**olieron**

ducharse

doo-CHAR-se (*v.*): to take a shower

"*Do charge* extra for how long they *shower*,"
says Leona Hells. "Guests suck out all the power!"

PRESENT TENSE		PRETERITE TENSE	
Yo	me ducho	Yo	me duché
Tú	te duchas	Tú	te duchaste
Él/Ella/Ud.	se ducha	Él/Ella/Ud.	se duchó
Nosotros	nos duchamos	Nosotros	nos duchamos
Vosotros	os ducháis	Vosotros	os duchasteis
Ellos/Ellas/Uds.	se duchan	Ellos/Ellas/Uds.	se ducharon

morir

mo-REER (*v.*): to die

**The lab mouse suffered from the weight of _more ear_—
without an ear trim it might _die_ in a year.**

PRESENT TENSE		PRETERITE TENSE	
Yo	muero	Yo	morí
Tú	mueres	Tú	moriste
Él/Ella/Ud.	muere	Él/Ella/Ud.	murió
Nosotros	morimos	Nosotros	morimos
Vosotros	morís	Vosotros	moristeis
Ellos/Ellas/Uds.	mueren	Ellos/Ellas/Uds.	murieron

cruzar

kroo-SAR (*v.*): to cross

**The magical _cruise our_ family takes
will _cross_ all seven seas and even ten lakes.**

PRESENT TENSE		PRETERITE TENSE	
Yo	**cruzo**	Yo	**crucé**
Tú	**cruzas**	Tú	**cruzaste**
Él/Ella/Ud.	**cruza**	Él/Ella/Ud.	**cruzó**
Nosotros	**cruzamos**	Nosotros	**cruzamos**
Vosotros	**cruzáis**	Vosotros	**cruzasteis**
Ellos/Ellas/Uds.	**cruzan**	Ellos/Ellas/Uds.	**cruzaron**

mandar

man-DAR (*v.*): to send

The <u>man dared</u> the hiker *to send*
his hiking boot out to the cliff's end.

PRESENT TENSE		PRETERITE TENSE	
Yo	mando	Yo	mandé
Tú	mandas	Tú	mandaste
Él/Ella/Ud.	manda	Él/Ella/Ud.	mandó
Nosotros	mandamos	Nosotros	mandamos
Vosotros	mandáis	Vosotros	mandasteis
Ellos/Ellas/Uds.	mandan	Ellos/Ellas/Uds.	mandaron

faltar

fal-TAR (*v.*): to be missing, to be lacking

When he saw the priest was *missing*,
the groom began to *falter* and start hissing.

PRESENT TENSE		PRETERITE TENSE	
Yo	falto	Yo	falté
Tú	faltas	Tú	faltaste
Él/Ella/Ud.	falta	Él/Ella/Ud.	faltó
Nosotros	faltamos	Nosotros	faltamos
Vosotros	faltáis	Vosotros	faltasteis
Ellos/Ellas/Uds.	faltan	Ellos/Ellas/Uds.	faltaron

temer

te–MER (*v.*): to fear

Nothing is funnier than a *timid bear*;
just stick out your tongue and he'll quake with *fear*.

PRESENT TENSE		PRETERITE TENSE	
Yo	temo	Yo	temí
Tú	temes	Tú	temiste
Él/Ella/Ud.	teme	Él/Ella/Ud.	temió
Nosotros	tememos	Nosotros	temimos
Vosotros	teméis	Vosotros	temisteis
Ellos/Ellas/Uds.	temen	Ellos/Ellas/Uds.	temieron

DRILL 11

Refresh Your Memory

Match the word and link to its corresponding definition.

1. preocuparse (preoccupied)
2. divertirse (diversion)
3. coser (closer)
4. oler (olé!)
5. ducharse (do charge … says)
6. morir (more ear)
7. cruzar (cruise our)
8. mandar (man dared)
9. faltar (falter)
10. temer (timid bear)

A. to cross
B. to fear
C. to take a shower
D. to amuse, distract (have a good time)
E. to smell
F. to worry
G. to be missing, to be lacking
H. to die
I. to send
J. to sew

Test Your Knowledge

Fill in the blanks with the present tense of the appropriate verb, except where indicated.

1. Ana, ¿ _____ [preterite] cuando fuimos a circo?

2. Nuestra madre _____ cuando no regresamos pronto a casa.

3. Muchachos, ¿ _____ algo raro? ¿Apagaron el gas?

4. Si quieres ser sastre, tienes que aprender a _____ .

5. Después del partido de fútbol, los chicos _____ [preterite] y se prepararon para la cena.

6. Los niños miraron en ambas direcciones cuando _____ [preterite] la calle.

7. Cristóbal Colón _____ [preterite] en el año 1506.

8. Nosotras _____ [preterite] a Teodoro a comprar huevos.

9. Yo _____ que haya olvidado las llaves en el carro.

10. ¿Tenemos todos los ingredientes, o nos _____ algo?

andar

an-DAR (*v.*): to walk

**The alien _android_ from planet Blegs
walks with wheels instead of legs.**

PRESENT TENSE		PRETERITE TENSE	
Yo	ando	Yo	anduve
Tú	andas	Tú	anduviste
Él/Ella/Ud.	anda	Él/Ella/Ud.	anduvo
Nosotros	andamos	Nosotros	anduvimos
Vosotros	andáis	Vosotros	anduvisteis
Ellos/Ellas/Uds.	andan	Ellos/Ellas/Uds.	anduvieron

oír

o-EER (*v.*): to hear

"Come closer, my dear," said old man Lear.
"These _old ears_ can barely *hear*."

PRESENT TENSE		PRETERITE TENSE	
Yo	oigo	Yo	oí
Tú	oyes	Tú	oíste
Él/Ella/Ud.	oye	Él/Ella/Ud.	oyó
Nosotros	oímos	Nosotros	oímos
Vosotros	oís	Vosotros	oísteis
Ellos/Ellas/Uds.	oyen	Ellos/Ellas/Uds.	oyeron

construir

kon–stroo–EER (*v.*): to build

The foreman developed a *construction fear*:
He'd stop *building* whenever a bulldozer came near.

PRESENT TENSE	
Yo	construyo
Tú	construyes
Él/Ella/Ud.	construye
Nosotros	construimos
Vosotros	construís
Ellos/Ellas/Uds.	construyen

PRETERITE TENSE	
Yo	construí
Tú	construiste
Él/Ella/Ud.	construyó
Nosotros	construimos
Vosotros	construisteis
Ellos/Ellas/Uds.	construyeron

bailar

bai-LAR (*v.*): to dance

**Kimmy had to _buy large_ shoes
to dance with her troupe of kangaroos.**

PRESENT TENSE	
Yo	**bailo**
Tú	**bailas**
Él/Ella/Ud.	**baila**
Nosotros	**bailamos**
Vosotros	**bailáis**
Ellos/Ellas/Uds.	**bailan**

PRETERITE TENSE	
Yo	**bailé**
Tú	**bailaste**
Él/Ella/Ud.	**bailó**
Nosotros	**bailamos**
Vosotros	**bailasteis**
Ellos/Ellas/Uds.	**bailaron**

mezclar

me-SKLAR (*v.*): to mix

**When the child *mixed* the red and black finger paint,
he created a *mess* of *color* that made his teacher faint.**

PRESENT TENSE		PRETERITE TENSE	
Yo	mezclo	Yo	mezclé
Tú	mezclas	Tú	mezclaste
Él/Ella/Ud.	mezcla	Él/Ella/Ud.	mezcló
Nosotros	mezclamos	Nosotros	mezclamos
Vosotros	mezcláis	Vosotros	mezclasteis
Ellos/Ellas/Uds.	mezclan	Ellos/Ellas/Uds.	mezclaron

bromear

bro-me-AR (*v.*): to joke, jest, make fun, ridicule

Jerry *joked* that a *broom* was the *mayor's* toy:
Sweeping issues away was what he seemed to enjoy.

PRESENT TENSE		**PRETERITE TENSE**	
Yo	bromeo	Yo	bromeé
Tú	bromeas	Tú	bromeaste
Él/Ella/Ud.	bromea	Él/Ella/Ud.	bromeó
Nosotros	bromeamos	Nosotros	bromeamos
Vosotros	broméais	Vosotros	bromeasteis
Ellos/Ellas/Uds.	bromean	Ellos/Ellas/Uds.	bromearon

nacer

na–SER (*v.*): to be born

"*No, Sir,*" he said to the king with a frown.
"A girl has been *born*—she won't inherit the crown."

PRESENT TENSE		PRETERITE TENSE	
Yo	**nazco**	Yo	**nací**
Tú	**naces**	Tú	**naciste**
Él/Ella/Ud.	**nace**	Él/Ella/Ud.	**nació**
Nosotros	**nacemos**	Nosotros	**nacimos**
Vosotros	**nacéis**	Vosotros	**nacisteis**
Ellos/Ellas/Uds.	**nacen**	Ellos/Ellas/Uds.	**nacieron**

limpiar

leem-pee-AR (*v.*): to clean

Sensing that the end was near, the sailor *cleaned* his boat and *limped* off the *pier*.

PRESENT TENSE		PRETERITE TENSE	
Yo	limpio	Yo	limpié
Tú	limpias	Tú	limpiaste
Él/Ella/Ud.	limpia	Él/Ella/Ud.	limpió
Nosotros	limpiamos	Nosotros	limpiamos
Vosotros	limpiáis	Vosotros	limpiasteis
Ellos/Ellas/Uds.	limpian	Ellos/Ellas/Uds.	limpiaron

permitir

per-mee-TEER (*v.*): to allow

**No crying is *allowed* by the hardy pioneers:
The strict rules of the trail don't *permit tears*.**

PRESENT TENSE		PRETERITE TENSE	
Yo	**permito**	Yo	**permití**
Tú	**permites**	Tú	**permitiste**
Él/Ella/Ud.	**permite**	Él/Ella/Ud.	**permitió**
Nosotros	**permitimos**	Nosotros	**permitimos**
Vosotros	**permitís**	Vosotros	**permitisteis**
Ellos/Ellas/Uds.	**permiten**	Ellos/Ellas/Uds.	**permitieron**

volar

vo–LAR (*v.*): to fly (a plane)

"You can't *fly*," said the soldier.
"You've got a bomb in your *molar*."

PRESENT TENSE		PRETERITE TENSE	
Yo	**vuelo**	Yo	**volé**
Tú	**vuelas**	Tú	**volaste**
Él/Ella/Ud.	**vuela**	Él/Ella/Ud.	**voló**
Nosotros	**volamos**	Nosotros	**volamos**
Vosotros	**voláis**	Vosotros	**volasteis**
Ellos/Ellas/Uds.	**vuelan**	Ellos/Ellas/Uds.	**volaron**

DRILL 12

Refresh Your Memory

Match the word and link to its corresponding definition.

1. andar (android)
2. oír (old ears)
3. construir (construction fear)
4. bailar (buy large)
5. mezclar (mess ... color)
6. bromear (broom ... mayor's)
7. nacer (no, Sir)
8. limpiar (limped ... pier)
9. permitir (permit tears)
10. volar (molar)

A. to joke, jest, make fun, ridicule
B. to fly (a plane)
C. to mix
D. to hear
E. to be born
F. to allow
G. to walk
H. to dance
I. to build
J. to clean

Test Your Knowledge

Fill in the blanks with the present tense of the appropriate verb, except where indicated.

1. Mi padre _____ [preterite] esta casa hace veinte años.

2. Espero que nuestro capitán sepa _____ bien el avión.

3. Carolina, ¿ _____ [preterite] ese ruido? ¿Qué será?

4. Martín y yo fuimos a una discoteca y _____ [preterite] toda la noche.

5. Si tú _____ esos dos químicos, puede haber una explosión.

6. El bebé ya no gatea. Ahora puede _____ .

7. Según la Biblia, el niño Jesús _____ [preterite] el 25 de diciembre.

8. A mi hermano le gusta mucho _____ : por eso tiene el apodo "el payaso."

9. Señora Larrea, ¿me _____ usar su baño?

10. Emilia y Juan Carlos, ¿ _____ [preterite] también la cocina?

nadar

na-DAR (*v.*): to swim

**Tim jumped in the _nasty, dark_ lake for a *swim*,
causing him to break many a limb.**

PRESENT TENSE		PRETERITE TENSE	
Yo	**nado**	Yo	**nadé**
Tú	**nadas**	Tú	**nadaste**
Él/Ella/Ud.	**nada**	Él/Ella/Ud.	**nadó**
Nosotros	**nadamos**	Nosotros	**nadamos**
Vosotros	**nadáis**	Vosotros	**nadasteis**
Ellos/Ellas/Uds.	**nadan**	Ellos/Ellas/Uds.	**nadaron**

abrazar

a–bra–SAR (*v.*): to hug, embrace

Bears are **known** *to hug* **each other:**
No one shows more love than a bear to its mother.

PRESENT TENSE		PRETERITE TENSE	
Yo	abrazo	Yo	abracé
Tú	abrazas	Tú	abrazaste
Él/Ella/Ud.	abraza	Él/Ella/Ud.	abrazó
Nosotros	abrazamos	Nosotros	abrazamos
Vosotros	abrazáis	Vosotros	abrazasteis
Ellos/Ellas/Uds.	abrazan	Ellos/Ellas/Uds.	abrazaron

cocinar

ko-see-NAR (*v.*): to cook

Guido worked the _casino_, taking care of the crooks, but his dream job was to open a restaurant and *cook*.

PRESENT TENSE		PRETERITE TENSE	
Yo	cocino	Yo	cociné
Tú	cocinas	Tú	cocinaste
Él/Ella/Ud.	cocina	Él/Ella/Ud.	cocinó
Nosotros	cocinamos	Nosotros	cocinamos
Vosotros	cocináis	Vosotros	cocinasteis
Ellos/Ellas/Uds.	cocinan	Ellos/Ellas/Uds.	cocinaron

ayudar

a-yoo-DAR (*v.*): to help

Anyone can *help* Rapunzel escape the witch's lair,
but don't *you dare* cut her hair.

PRESENT TENSE		PRETERITE TENSE	
Yo	ayudo	Yo	ayudé
Tú	ayudas	Tú	ayudaste
Él/Ella/Ud.	ayuda	Él/Ella/Ud.	ayudó
Nosotros	ayudamos	Nosotros	ayudamos
Vosotros	ayudáis	Vosotros	ayudasteis
Ellos/Ellas/Uds.	ayudan	Ellos/Ellas/Uds.	ayudaron

haber

a-BER (*v.*): to have, there be

A bear has **no winter cares
in his hibernation lairs.**

PRESENT TENSE		PRETERITE TENSE	
Yo	he	Yo	hube
Tú	has	Tú	hubiste
Él/Ella/Ud.	ha/hay	Él/Ella/Ud.	hubo
Nosotros	hemos	Nosotros	hubimos
Vosotros	habéis	Vosotros	hubisteis
Ellos/Ellas/Uds.	han	Ellos/Ellas/Uds.	hubieron

sentirse

sen-TEER-se (*v.*): to feel

Jeremy's lover has quickly departed;
He _sends tears away_, but he *feels* brokenhearted.

PRESENT TENSE		PRETERITE TENSE	
Yo	me siento	Yo	me sentí
Tú	te sientes	Tú	te sentiste
Él/Ella/Ud.	se siente	Él/Ella/Ud.	se sintió
Nosotros	nos sentimos	Nosotros	nos sentimos
Vosotros	os sentís	Vosotros	os sentisteis
Ellos/Ellas/Uds.	se sienten	Ellos/Ellas/Uds.	se sintieron

doler

do–LER (**v.**): to ache, hurt

The baker was *hurt* when his *dough lair* was raided,
and the ache from the bruise still hasn't faded.

PRESENT TENSE		PRETERITE TENSE	
Yo	**duelo**	Yo	**dolí**
Tú	**dueles**	Tú	**doliste**
Él/Ella/Ud.	**duele**	Él/Ella/Ud.	**dolió**
Nosotros	**dolemos**	Nosotros	**dolimos**
Vosotros	**doléis**	Vosotros	**dolisteis**
Ellos/Ellas/Uds.	**duelen**	Ellos/Ellas/Uds.	**dolieron**

parar

pa-RAR (**v.**): to stop, halt

When Ma drives the car, *Pa roars* for her *to stop*;
because she drives so fast, she doesn't see the cop.

PRESENT TENSE		PRETERITE TENSE	
Yo	**paro**	Yo	**paré**
Tú	**paras**	Tú	**paraste**
Él/Ella/Ud.	**para**	Él/Ella/Ud.	**paró**
Nosotros	**paramos**	Nosotros	**paramos**
Vosotros	**paráis**	Vosotros	**parasteis**
Ellos/Ellas/Uds.	**paran**	Ellos/Ellas/Uds.	**pararon**

planchar

plan–CHAR (*v.*): to iron

Neil didn't *plan* to *char* his pants,
but he probably shouldn't have tried *to iron* and dance.

PRESENT TENSE		PRETERITE TENSE	
Yo	**plancho**	Yo	**planché**
Tú	**planchas**	Tú	**planchaste**
Él/Ella/Ud.	**plancha**	Él/Ella/Ud.	**planchó**
Nosotros	**planchamos**	Nosotros	**planchamos**
Vosotros	**plancháis**	Vosotros	**planchasteis**
Ellos/Ellas/Uds.	**planchan**	Ellos/Ellas/Uds.	**plancharon**

cocer al horno

co-SER al OR-no (**v.**): to bake

Al never *baked* for his wife until his pal told him true:
"*Cook for her Al, or no* more kisses for you."

<table>
<tr><td colspan="2">PRESENT TENSE</td><td colspan="2">PRETERITE TENSE</td></tr>
<tr><td>Yo</td><td>cuezo al horno</td><td>Yo</td><td>cocí al horno</td></tr>
<tr><td>Tú</td><td>cueces al horno</td><td>Tú</td><td>cociste al horno</td></tr>
<tr><td>Él/Ella/Ud.</td><td>cuece al horno</td><td>Él/Ella/Ud.</td><td>coció al horno</td></tr>
<tr><td>Nosotros</td><td>cocemos al horno</td><td>Nosotros</td><td>cocimos al horno</td></tr>
<tr><td>Vosotros</td><td>cocéis al horno</td><td>Vosotros</td><td>cocisteis al horno</td></tr>
<tr><td>Ellos/Ellas/Uds.</td><td>cuecen al horno</td><td>Ellos/Ellas/Uds.</td><td>cocieron al horno</td></tr>
</table>

DRILL 13

Refresh Your Memory

Match the word and link to its corresponding definition.

1. nadar (nasty, dark)
2. abrazar (bears are)
3. cocinar (casino)
4. ayudar (you dare)
5. haber (a bear)
6. sentirse (sends tears away)
7. doler (dough lair)
8. parar (Pa roars)
9. planchar (plan … char)
10. cocer al horno (cook for her Al, or no)

A. to iron
B. to swim
C. to have, there be
D. to cook
E. to ache, hurt
F. to hug, embrace
G. to feel
H. to help
I. to bake
J. to stop, halt

Test Your Knowledge

Fill in the blanks with the present tense of the appropriate verb, except where indicated.

1. No puedes _____ en esa agua: es demasiado fría.

2. Jaime _____ [preterite] muy mal cuando vio perder su equipo.

3. Nunca me ha gustado _____: prefiero salir a comer.

4. Antes de irse, el soldado _____ [preterite] a su madre y le dijo que volvería pronto.

5. Martín nos _____ [preterite] a pintar la casa.

6. _____ dos ratones escondidos detrás de la nevera.

7. ¿Te _____ [preterite] mucho la inyección?

8. Mi mejor amiga y yo charlamos por tres horas, sin _____.

9. Cristina siempre _____ galletas, pasteles y panes.

10. Yo _____ [preterite] tres camisas y una falda.

colgar

kol–GAR (*v.*): to hang up

The *cold guard* *hung up* his coat,
although he was freezing, he wanted to gloat.

PRESENT TENSE		PRETERITE TENSE	
Yo	cuelgo	Yo	colgué
Tú	cuelgas	Tú	colgaste
Él/Ella/Ud.	cuelga	Él/Ella/Ud.	colgó
Nosotros	colgamos	Nosotros	colgamos
Vosotros	colgáis	Vosotros	colgasteis
Ellos/Ellas/Uds.	cuelgan	Ellos/Ellas/Uds.	colgaron

calentar

ka-len-TAR (*v.*): to heat

**Kooky Kal's <u>calendar</u> said it was almost July—
time *to heat* up the oven and make berry pie.**

PRESENT TENSE		PRETERITE TENSE	
Yo	**caliento**	Yo	**calenté**
Tú	**calientas**	Tú	**calentaste**
Él/Ella/Ud.	**calienta**	Él/Ella/Ud.	**calentó**
Nosotros	**calentamos**	Nosotros	**calentamos**
Vosotros	**calentáis**	Vosotros	**calentasteis**
Ellos/Ellas/Uds.	**calientan**	Ellos/Ellas/Uds.	**calentaron**

caerse

ka-ER-se (*v.*): to fall

Sky Air says their planes *fall* out of the sky—
perhaps it's one airline you don't want to fly!

PRESENT TENSE		PRETERITE TENSE	
Yo	caigo	Yo	caí
Tú	caes	Tú	caíste
Él/Ella/Ud.	cae	Él/Ella/Ud.	cayó
Nosotros	caemos	Nosotros	caímos
Vosotros	caéis	Vosotros	caísteis
Ellos/Ellas/Uds.	caen	Ellos/Ellas/Uds.	cayeron

afeitarse

a-fei-TAR-se **(v.)**: to shave

Jim didn't think he was _a fainter_; he _said_ he was bold,
until he cut himself _shaving_ and passed out cold.

PRESENT TENSE	
Yo	me afeito
Tú	te afeitas
Él/Ella/Ud.	se afeita
Nosotros	nos afeitamos
Vosotros	os afeitáis
Ellos/Ellas/Uds.	se afeitan

PRETERITE TENSE	
Yo	me afeité
Tú	te afeitaste
Él/Ella/Ud.	se afeitó
Nosotros	nos afeitamos
Vosotros	os afeitasteis
Ellos/Ellas/Uds.	se afeitaron

prestar

pre-STAR (*v.*): to lend

The magician won't *lend* his <u>*presto*</u> stick,
because without it he can't even do one trick.

PRESENT TENSE		PRETERITE TENSE	
Yo	**presto**	Yo	**presté**
Tú	**prestas**	Tú	**prestaste**
Él/Ella/Ud.	**presta**	Él/Ella/Ud.	**prestó**
Nosotros	**prestamos**	Nosotros	**prestamos**
Vosotros	**prestáis**	Vosotros	**prestasteis**
Ellos/Ellas/Uds.	**prestan**	Ellos/Ellas/Uds.	**prestaron**

acostarse

a-ko-STAR-se **(v.): to go to bed**

Our costar said that after the play,
she must *go to bed* because she had a long day.

PRESENT TENSE		PRETERITE TENSE	
Yo	me acuesto	Yo	me acosté
Tú	te acuestas	Tú	te acostaste
Él/Ella/Ud.	se acuesta	Él/Ella/Ud.	se acostó
Nosotros	nos acostamos	Nosotros	nos acostamos
Vosotros	os acostáis	Vosotros	os acostasteis
Ellos/Ellas/Uds.	se acuestan	Ellos/Ellas/Uds.	se acostaron

maquillarse

ma–kee–YAR–se (*v.*): to put on makeup

Outside, the *marquee says* the starlet's name;
inside, she *puts on her makeup* and hopes for fame.

PRESENT TENSE		PRETERITE TENSE	
Yo	me maquillo	Yo	me maquillé
Tú	te maquillas	Tú	te maquillaste
Él/Ella/Ud.	se maquilla	Él/Ella/Ud.	se maquilló
Nosotros	nos maquillamos	Nosotros	nos maquillamos
Vosotros	os maquilláis	Vosotros	os maquillasteis
Ellos/Ellas/Uds.	se maquillan	Ellos/Ellas/Uds.	se maquillaron

apoyar

a-po-YAR (*v.*): to support

"*Aww, poor yard*," said Beth, "You're totally weeds! I've got to *support* you and buy some new seeds."

PRESENT TENSE		PRETERITE TENSE	
Yo	**apoyo**	Yo	**apoyé**
Tú	**apoyas**	Tú	**apoyaste**
Él/Ella/Ud.	**apoya**	Él/Ella/Ud.	**apoyó**
Nosotros	**apoyamos**	Nosotros	**apoyamos**
Vosotros	**apoyáis**	Vosotros	**apoyasteis**
Ellos/Ellas/Uds.	**apoyan**	Ellos/Ellas/Uds.	**apoyaron**

llamar

ya-MAR (*v.*): to call

"*Call ya ma*," was my mom's tireless refrain.
She had to nag my dad, or he'd never call grandma Jane.

PRESENT TENSE		PRETERITE TENSE	
Yo	llamo	Yo	llamé
Tú	llamas	Tú	llamaste
Él/Ella/Ud.	llama	Él/Ella/Ud.	llamó
Nosotros	llamamos	Nosotros	llamamos
Vosotros	llamáis	Vosotros	llamasteis
Ellos/Ellas/Uds.	llaman	Ellos/Ellas/Uds.	llamaron

llenar

ye-NAR (**v.**): to fill

Oliver is an optimist, _rain or_ shine:
"The glass is half-_full_" is his favorite line.

PRESENT TENSE		PRETERITE TENSE	
Yo	lleno	Yo	llené
Tú	llenas	Tú	llenaste
Él/Ella/Ud.	llena	Él/Ella/Ud.	llenó
Nosotros	llenamos	Nosotros	llenamos
Vosotros	llenáis	Vosotros	llenasteis
Ellos/Ellas/Uds.	llenan	Ellos/Ellas/Uds.	llenaron

DRILL 14

Refresh Your Memory

Match the word and link to its corresponding definition.

1.	colgar (cold guard)	A.	to shave
2.	calentar (calendar)	B.	to put on makeup
3.	caerse (Sky Air says)	C.	to heat
4.	afeitarse (a fainter … said)	D.	to hang up
5.	prestar (presto)	E.	to go to bed
6.	acostarse (our costar said)	F.	to fall
7.	maquillarse (marquee says)	G.	to call
8.	apoyar (aww, poor yard)	H.	to lend
9.	llamar (ya ma)	I.	to fill
10.	llenar (rain or)	J.	to support

Test Your Knowledge

Fill in the blanks with the present tense of the appropriate verb, except where indicated.

1. Nosotros _____ [preterite] la sopa en el microondas.

2. Cuando el bebé _____ [preterite] de la silla, empezó a llorar.

3. Si no _____ tus camisas, se te van a arrugar.

4. Mi padre tiene que _____ la cara todos los días: sino, se le crece la barba.

5. Cuando estaba enferma, tuve que _____ muy temprano.

6. Le _____ [preterite] a Federico mi calculadora: espero que no la haya perdido.

7. La señorita se vistió, _____ [preterite], y salió a cenar con su novio.

8. Ayer Berta _____ [preterite] por teléfono a Matilde.

9. Tengo que _____ el tanque con gas.

10. Tu eres un gran amigo: siempre me _____.

despegar

de-spe-GAR (*v.*): to take off

When her plane *takes off*, Natalie feels _desperate_:
She gets so nervous, she's sure she'll crash in it.

PRESENT TENSE		PRETERITE TENSE	
Yo	despego	Yo	despegué
Tú	despegas	Tú	despegaste
Él/Ella/Ud.	despega	Él/Ella/Ud.	despegó
Nosotros	despegamos	Nosotros	despegamos
Vosotros	despegáis	Vosotros	despegasteis
Ellos/Ellas/Uds.	despegan	Ellos/Ellas/Uds.	despegaron

esconder

e-skon-DER **(v.)**: to hide

The lawyer wanted *to hide* when his *ex's scandal* broke because everyone would think his career was a joke.

PRESENT TENSE		PRETERITE TENSE	
Yo	**escondo**	Yo	**escondí**
Tú	**escondes**	Tú	**escondiste**
Él/Ella/Ud.	**esconde**	Él/Ella/Ud.	**escondió**
Nosotros	**escondemos**	Nosotros	**escondimos**
Vosotros	**escondéis**	Vosotros	**escondisteis**
Ellos/Ellas/Uds.	**esconden**	Ellos/Ellas/Uds.	**escondieron**

derretir

de-re-TEER (**v.**): to melt

**Derrick _dared_ to let _a tear_ fall
when he saw ice cream _melt_ at the county fair stall.**

PRESENT TENSE		PRETERITE TENSE	
Yo	**derrito**	Yo	**derretí**
Tú	**derrites**	Tú	**derretiste**
Él/Ella/Ud.	**derrite**	Él/Ella/Ud.	**derritió**
Nosotros	**derretimos**	Nosotros	**derretimos**
Vosotros	**derretís**	Vosotros	**derretisteis**
Ellos/Ellas/Uds.	**derriten**	Ellos/Ellas/Uds.	**derritieron**

gastar

ga-STAR (*v.*): to spend

Gary *spent* so much money putting *gas* in his *car*,
he decided to start roller-skating near and far.

PRESENT TENSE		PRETERITE TENSE	
Yo	gasto	Yo	gasté
Tú	gastas	Tú	gastaste
Él/Ella/Ud.	gasta	Él/Ella/Ud.	gastó
Nosotros	gastamos	Nosotros	gastamos
Vosotros	gastáis	Vosotros	gastasteis
Ellos/Ellas/Uds.	gastan	Ellos/Ellas/Uds.	gastaron

lanzar

lan-SAR (*v.*): to throw

**Jerry *threw* a snowball into the _Lands of Czar_—
he hit Ivan's head, and Ivan saw stars.**

PRESENT TENSE		PRETERITE TENSE	
Yo	**lanzo**	Yo	**lancé**
Tú	**lanzas**	Tú	**lanzaste**
Él/Ella/Ud.	**lanza**	Él/Ella/Ud.	**lanzó**
Nosotros	**lanzamos**	Nosotros	**lanzamos**
Vosotros	**lanzáis**	Vosotros	**lanzasteis**
Ellos/Ellas/Uds.	**lanzan**	Ellos/Ellas/Uds.	**lanzaron**

patear

pa-te-AR (*v.*): to kick

**The boys keep *kicking Pattie's arse*,
but she doesn't get upset as it's just a farce.**

PRESENT TENSE		PRETERITE TENSE	
Yo	**pateo**	Yo	**pateé**
Tú	**pateas**	Tú	**pateaste**
Él/Ella/Ud.	**patea**	Él/Ella/Ud.	**pateó**
Nosotros	**pateamos**	Nosotros	**pateamos**
Vosotros	**pateáis**	Vosotros	**pateasteis**
Ellos/Ellas/Uds.	**patean**	Ellos/Ellas/Uds.	**patearon**

anular

a-noo-LAR (*v.*): to cancel

The doctor *cancelled* his _annual_ subscription
to the boring magazine, *All About Prescriptions*.

PRESENT TENSE		PRETERITE TENSE	
Yo	anulo	Yo	anulé
Tú	anulas	Tú	anulaste
Él/Ella/Ud.	anula	Él/Ella/Ud.	anuló
Nosotros	anulamos	Nosotros	anulamos
Vosotros	anuláis	Vosotros	anulasteis
Ellos/Ellas/Uds.	anulan	Ellos/Ellas/Uds.	anularon

atar

a-TAR (*v.*): to tie

**The campers scurried *to tie <u>a tarp</u>* over their tent
as snowball-size hail made its descent.**

PRESENT TENSE		PRETERITE TENSE	
Yo	**ato**	Yo	**até**
Tú	**atas**	Tú	**ataste**
Él/Ella/Ud.	**ata**	Él/Ella/Ud.	**ató**
Nosotros	**atamos**	Nosotros	**atamos**
Vosotros	**atáis**	Vosotros	**atasteis**
Ellos/Ellas/Uds.	**atan**	Ellos/Ellas/Uds.	**ataron**

peinarse

pei-NAR-se (*v.*): to comb one's hair

Want a *pain in the nursery***? Try** *to comb her hair*;
the baby really wishes her head were bare.

PRESENT TENSE		PRETERITE TENSE	
Yo	me peino	Yo	me peiné
Tú	te peinas	Tú	te peinaste
Él/Ella/Ud.	se peina	Él/Ella/Ud.	se peinó
Nosotros	nos peinamos	Nosotros	nos peinamos
Vosotros	os peináis	Vosotros	os peinasteis
Ellos/Ellas/Uds.	se peinan	Ellos/Ellas/Uds.	se peinaron

callarse

ka-YAR-se (*v.*): to shut up, be quiet

Jared's little brother was a _crier_, so he'd _say_,
"*Shut up* crybaby, or at least go away."

PRESENT TENSE		PRETERITE TENSE	
Yo	me callo	Yo	me callé
Tú	te callas	Tú	te callaste
Él/Ella/Ud.	se calla	Él/Ella/Ud.	se calló
Nosotros	nos callamos	Nosotros	nos callamos
Vosotros	os calláis	Vosotros	os callasteis
Ellos/Ellas/Uds.	se callan	Ellos/Ellas/Uds.	se callaron

DRILL 15

Refresh Your Memory

Match the word and link to its corresponding definition.

1. despegar (desperate)
2. esconder (ex's scandal)
3. derretir (dared ... a tear)
4. gastar (gas ... car)
5. lanzar (Lands of Czar)
6. patear (Pattie's arse)
7. anular (annual)
8. atar (a tarp)
9. peinarse (pain in the nursery)
10. callarse (crier ... say)

A. to throw
B. to take off
C. to comb one's hair
D. to spend
E. to cancel
F. to melt
G. to kick
H. to hide
I. to shut up, be quiet
J. to tie

Test Your Knowledge

Fill in the blanks with the present tense of the appropriate verb, except where indicated.

1. El drogadicto _____ [preterite] las drogas en un armario.

2. El perro de los vecinos nunca _____ : pasa todo el día ladrando.

3. Nosotros _____ [preterite] mucho dinero cuando fuimos a Las Vegas.

4. El avión _____ [preterite] a las diez de la mañana.

5. El caballero _____ [preterite] su espada contra el enemigo.

6. No puedo _____ la pelota: me rompí el dedo del pie.

7. La cera de la vela _____ [preterite] sobre la mesa.

8. Mi hijo todavía no sabe como _____ los cordones de sus zapatos.

9. Decidimos _____ el contrato: los dos nos habíamos cambiado de opinión.

10. Hoy no tengo ganas de _____ : me voy a poner una gorra de béisbol.

ADJECTIVES

aburrido (-a)

a–boo–REE–do/a (*adj.*): boring

Spicy foods made Bob's face glow,
so he had to order <u>a</u> boring <u>burrito</u>.

antipático (-a)

an-tee-PA-tee-ko/a (*adj.*): unsympathetic, unpleasant

**Miserable *Auntie Pattie*
is *unsympathetic* and batty.**

guapo (-a)

GWA-po/a (*adj.*): good-looking,
attractive

A *good-looking guava*
pleased the tribal king of Java.

bajo (-a)
BA-ho/a (*adj.*): short

A *short* <u>banjo</u> won a bow
at the International Banjo Show.

gordo (-a)
GOR-do/a (*adj.*): fat

Gordon the cat is much too *fat*.

lindo (-a)

LEEN-do/a *(adj.)*: pretty

**The *pretty limbo* star
brought her own pink limbo bar.**

joven

HO-ven *(adj.)*: young

The *young* girl, who really liked to bake,
only wanted an _oven_ so she could make a cake.

hablador (-a)

a–bla–DOR/a (*adj.*): talkative

Talkative **Ma bores quiet Pa;**
to him she sounds like "_Ha, ha, blah_, blah, blah."

bueno (-a)

BWE-no/a *(adj.)*: good

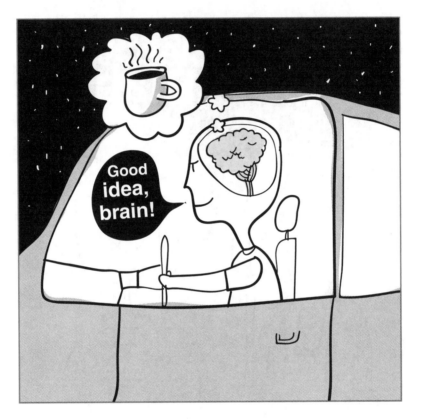

**A *good* *brain* *knows*
not to drive and doze.**

viejo (-a)

VYE-ho/a (*adj.*): old

"There's a *fee, eh? Hold* the door.
I'm too *old* to pay a lot at the casket store."

DRILL 16

Refresh Your Memory

Match the word and link to its corresponding definition.

1.	aburrido (–a) (a … burrito)	A.	short
2.	antipático (–a) (Auntie Pattie)	B.	good-looking, attractive
3.	guapo (–a) (guava)	C.	good
4.	bajo (–a) (banjo)	D.	young
5.	gordo (–a) (Gordon)	E.	unsympathetic, unpleasant
6.	lindo (–a) (limbo)	F.	pretty
7.	joven (oven)	G.	old
8.	hablador (–a) (ha, ha, blah)	H.	fat
9.	bueno (–a) (brain knows)	I.	talkative
10.	viejo (–a) (fee, eh? Hold)	J.	boring

Test Your Knowledge

Fill in the blanks with the appropriate adjective.

1. El brócoli es _____ para la salud.

2. La novia de Patricio es _____. Nos cae mal a todos porque tiene mal carácter.

3. Cuando Aníbal se vistió de terno, lucía muy _____.

4. La señora es _____. ¡Mide sólo 1.2 metros (4 pies)!

5. Este libro de historia es muy _____. ¡Me da sueño leerlo!

6. Generalmente, la gente _____ come demasiado.

7. ¿Tienes sólo 17 años? Eres aún _____.

8. El señor Cañizares me regaló una flor muy _____.

9. La abuela de Jaime es _____: tiene 93 años.

10. Mi suegra es muy _____: nunca se calla.

pobre

PO-bre *(adj.)*: poor

After losing his job, the _cobra_ was _poor_,
so to collect some money, he went door to door.

único (-a)

OO-nee-ko/a *(adj.)*: only

If it were real, the *unicorn*
would be the *only* horse with a magic horn.

grande

GRAN-de (*adj.*): big, large

Granny Day is a *large* celebration,
which honors grandmas from all the nation.

travieso (-a)

tra-VYE-so/a *(adj.)*: mischievous

He wasn't a criminal, but he *traveled, so*
he seemed *mischievous* to those he didn't know.

simpático (-a)

GRAN-de *(adj.)*: nice, pleasant

Sam's Patty Co. hires kids who are *nice*;
they want everyone who comes once to come twice.

pesado (-a)

pe-SA-do/a (*adj.*): heavy

"It *pays to do* the *heavy* work first,"
said the burly bricklayer to his helper, the clerk.

bonito (-a)

bo–NEE-to/a (*adj.*): pretty

Picky Pete wants to marry, but he had to say no.
"Betty's really *pretty*, but she's got a *bony toe*."

alto (-a)

AL-to/a (*adj.*): tall

The soccer player was *tall*, but that's not all:
He was also <u>all toe</u> and he never missed the ball.

pequeño (-a)

pe-KE-nyo/a (*adj.*): small

The farmer's *small* son wanted to learn and grow;
he would milk cows and mow lawns,
but would he *pick cane? No!*

delgado (-a)

del-GA-do/a (*adj.*): thin

The pizza at the *deli got dough* much too *thin*.
Therefore, no prizes for deep dish would it ever win.

DRILL 17

Refresh Your Memory

Match the word and link to its corresponding definition.

1. pobre (cobra)
2. único (–a) (unicorn)
3. grande (Granny Day)
4. travieso (–a) (traveled, so)
5. simpático (–a) (Sam's Patty Co.)
6. pesado (–a) (pays to do)
7. bonito (–a) (bony toe)
8. alto (–a) (all toe)
9. pequeño (–a) (pick cane? No!)
10. delgado (–a) (deli got dough)

A. big, large
B. heavy
C. poor
D. small
E. thin
F. only
G. mischievous
H. tall
I. pretty
J. nice, pleasant

Test Your Knowledge

Fill in the blanks with the appropriate adjective.

1. Es _____ tu abuela. Quisiera conversar más con ella.

2. La televisión que compramos era demasiado _____: la tuvimos que devolver porque no cabía en el armario.

3. Es nuestro deber ayudar a la gente _____ del mundo.

4. Mi cachorro no es malo, sino muy _____.

5. No podemos mover el mueble sin una carretilla: es muy _____.

6. Los jugadores de baloncesto suelen ser muy _____.

7. El vestido de la novia era muy _____. Claramente había costado mucho dinero.

8. Las raciones en ese restaurante son _____. Nunca satisfacen mi hambre.

9. Esta escultura es _____: no existe otra así.

10. Marta, estas tan _____. ¿Estás comiendo suficiente?

feo (-a)

FE-o/a (*adj.*): ugly

**Don't try to go to Pretty Town's beauty store:
If you're *ugly* there's a _fee owed_ at the door.**

cansado (-a)

kan-SA-do/a (*adj.*): tired

The *tired* carpenter is moving slow—
he can't saw wood, but he <u>can saw dough</u>.

caro (-a)

KA-ro/a *(adj.)*: expensive

In *Cairo* we saw King Tut's jewel;
it was so *expensive* it made all the women drool.

vacío (-a)

va-SEE-o/a (*adj.*): empty

The islanders swim in the *vast sea over* there;
it's *empty* of sharks so they can swim without a care.

triste

TREE-ste *(adj.)*: sad

In the winter *trees stay* in the ground,
even if they're *sad* and brown.

feliz

fe-LEES (*adj.*): happy

**Circus _fleas_ are the *happiest* bugs,
always laughing and administering hugs.**

embarazada

em-ba-ra-SA-da (*adj.*): pregnant

Susie was <u>*embarrassed*</u> to wear a swimsuit at the beach; because she was *pregnant*, she resembled a peach.

sucio (-a)

SOO-syo/a *(adj.)*: dirty

The *dirty* pockets of the *suit Sue owns*
are full of plastic bags with moldy scones.

ocupado (-a)

o-koo-PA-do/a *(adj.)*: busy

The squirrel was _occupied_ and *busy* for weeks,
stuffing acorns into his cheeks.

frío (-a)

FREE-o/a *(adj.)*: cold

In the *cold* when icicles grow on cowboys' coats,
all of their horses get a pail of *free oats*.

DRILL 18

Refresh Your Memory

Match the word and link to its corresponding definition.

1. feo (–a) (fee owed)
2. cansado (–a) (can saw dough)
3. caro (–a) (Cairo)
4. vacío (–a) (vast sea over)
5. triste (trees stay)
6. feliz (fleas)
7. embarazada (embarrassed)
8. sucio (–a) (suits Sue owns)
9. ocupado (–a) (occupied)
10. frío (–a) (free oats)

A. busy
B. sad
C. dirty
D. empty
E. happy
F. cold
G. tired
H. pregnant
I. ugly
J. expensive

Test Your Knowledge

Fill in the blanks with the appropriate adjective.

1. No me gusta el helado. La comida _____ me hace doler los dientes.

2. En la película, un monstruo muy _____ ataca a la ciudad.

3. La señora _____ esperaba gemelos.

4. ¿Prefieres esta chaqueta barata, o aquella más _____?

5. La botella está _____. Anoche terminamos el vino.

6. Se puso muy _____ cuando supo las malas noticias.

7. No te puedo ayudar en este momento. Estoy demasiado _____ con mi trabajo.

8. Juanito, ¡no toques la basura! ¡Es _____!

9. Después de la excursión al museo, todos estábamos _____. Sólo queríamos descansar.

10. Es un niño muy _____: siempre sonríe.

rico (-a)

REE-ko/a (*adj.*): rich

The *rich* society of women <u>reeked</u> of mold;
all of their money couldn't hide that they were old.

caliente

kal–YEN–te (*adj.*): hot

This summer, the chicken coop is so *hot* inside,
the eggs that *Cal's hens lay* all come out fried.

tranquilo (-a)

tran-KEE-lo/a (*adj.*): quiet, peaceful

The *trained quilters* quilted in a *quiet* spot
so they could focus on quilting little knitted knots.

loco (-a)

LO-ko/a (*adj.*): crazy

"*Lower, Cohen*! You're flying too high!"
said the *crazy* old bat to her friend, the fly.

fastidioso (-a)

fa-stee-DYO-so/a (*adj.*): annoying

Dumping Karl was an idea with which they were toying—
the band found his catchphrase, "*fat idiot*," *annoying*.

nuevo (-a)

NWE-vo/a (*adj.*): new

The brave *new* surfer can't wait to get wet.
He paddles out through the surf but sees *no wave* yet.

enfermo (-a)

en-FER-mo/a *(adj.)*: sick

When *sick* with an ache, Trish ran to the *infirmary*;
the nurse diagnosed it as bronchopulmonary.

débil

DE-beel (*adj.*): weak

The <u>*devil*</u>'s powers eventually got *weak*
as he was defeated by a strong, angelic geek.

cómico (-a)

KO-mee-ko/a (*adj.*): funny

**Everyone thought the _comic_ was _funny_,
so he walked out of the nightclub with a pile of money.**

barato (-a)

ba-RAT-o/a (*adj.*): cheap

The *bar rat* always orders *cheap* drinks,
knocks them back quickly, and into his seat he sinks.

DRILL 19

Refresh Your Memory

Match the word and link to its corresponding definition.

1. rico (–a) (reeked)
2. caliente (Cal's hens lay)
3. tranquilo (–a) (trained quilters)
4. loco (–a) (lower, Cohen)
5. fastidioso (–a) (fat idiot)
6. nuevo (–a) (no wave)
7. enfermo (–a) (infirmary)
8. débil (devil)
9. cómico (–a) (comic)
10. barato (–a) (bar rat)

A. rich
B. annoying
C. funny
D. hot
E. cheap
F. crazy
G. sick
H. quiet, peaceful
I. weak
J. new

Test Your Knowledge

Fill in the blanks with the appropriate adjective.

1. El café está muy _____. Te puede quemar.
2. Mi tío es _____: tiene bastante dinero.
3. El hospital está lleno de gente _____.
4. Romeo estaba _____ de amor por Julieta.
5. Es muy _____ madrugar todas la mañanas.
6. Vendimos el carro viejo y compramos uno _____.
7. El doctor recomienda que descanses en un lugar _____.
8. Teodoro nos cuenta chistes muy _____.
9. Después del maratón, Jaime se sentía _____ y cansado.
10. Las marcas nacionales son más _____ que aquellas importadas.

claro (-a)

KLA-o/a *(adj.)*: bright, light, clear

Her entrance was stunning and her singing was *bright*;
Clare O.'s the next Idol as sure as night.

fuerte

FWER-te (*adj.*): strong

The warlocks made a *fur tea*, and it was a *strong* brew;
wherever you applied it, thick hair grew.

torpe

TOR-pe (*adj.*): clumsy

The *clumsy* pilot accidentally launched the *torpedo* and scrambled to shout, "Look out below!"

gratis

GRA-tees *(adj.)*: free (no charge)

The guy at the yard sale said the shirts were *free*,
so Dave ran to the rack and began to *gra*b *tees*.

ruidoso (-a)

rwee-DO-so/a (*adj.*): loud, noisy

Deb had to bake bread far from the *noisy* crowd—
she'd get *ruined dough* if the room was too loud.

mezquino (-a)

me–SKEE–no/a (*adj.*): mean, stingy

The friendly *mosquito* didn't want to be *mean*,
but his bites were the only way he could be seen.

orgulloso (-a)

or-goo-YO-so/a *(adj.)*: proud

The old doctor told a young surgeon he knows,
"Be *proud* of every <u>organ you sew</u>."

verdadero (-a)

ver-da-DE-ro/a *(adj.)*: true

The movie star's daughter knew the
version **her** *dad wrote* **was** *true***,**
but about her mother's version, she hadn't a clue.

estrecho (-a)

e-STRE-cho/a **(*adj.*): narrow**

In far-away Italy, down a *narrow*, winding lane,
you'll find you can *easily stretch* without any pain.

perezoso (-a)

pe-re-SO-so/a (*adj.*): lazy

Mathilda was *lazy* about buying gifts for her nieces:
Her *pair of so-so* puzzles were missing pieces.

DRILL 20

Refresh Your Memory

Match the word and link to its corresponding definition.

1. claro (–a) (Clare O.)
2. fuerte (fur tea)
3. torpe (torpedo)
4. gratis (grab tees)
5. ruidoso (–a) (ruined dough)
6. mezquino (–a) (mosquito)
7. orgulloso (–a) (organ you sew)
8. verdadero (–a) (version … dad wrote)
9. estrecho (–a) (easily stretch)
10. perezoso (–a) (pair of so-so)

A. proud
B. clumsy
C. light, clear, bright
D. free (no charge)
E. lazy
F. loud, noisy
G. mean, stingy
H. strong
I. true
J. narrow

Test Your Knowledge

Fill in the blanks with the appropriate adjective.

1. Los borrachos suelen ser _____.

2. Los loros de la vecina son muy _____: hacen mucho ruido cuando charlan.

3. Ese pasaje es demasiado _____ para mi camioneta. Tenemos que cambiar la ruta.

4. El dueño de la fábrica es _____. Trata mal a sus empleados.

5. En este almacén si compras dos camisas, recibes la tercera _____.

6. Cuando me gradué de la universidad, mis padres estaban _____ de mí.

7. Para ser un buen leñador, tienes que ser _____.

8. Los diamantes finos son más _____ que aquellos baratos.

9. Mi hermano mayor es _____: prefiere dormir que ayudar con los quehaceres de la casa.

10. Los amigos _____ nunca te dejan solo.

ADVERBS

sencillamente

sen-see-ya-MEN-te *(adv.)*: simple, in a
straightforward manner

The practical jokester's *sensible* attack:
Send silly men tea that dyes their lips black.

difícilmente

dee–FEE–seel–men–te **(adv.)**: hardly,
scarcely; with difficulty

It is *difficult* to get by
with *hardly* any pie.

rápidamente

RA-pee-da-men-te (*adv.*): quickly

Rapidly feeling sickly,
Ruth got a thermometer *quickly*.

aquí

a-KEE (*adv.*): here

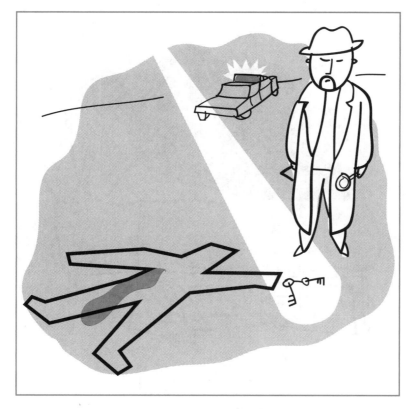

Just as the detective feared,
a key for the hotel room is _here_.

debajo

de-BA-ho (*adv.*): underneath

A very dead _Deb_ kept her head
***underneath* the neatly made bed.**

mal

mal (*adj.*): bad

The *bad* teenagers wanted to go to the *mall*
to smash up some windows and scare someone small.

así

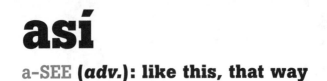

a–SEE (*adv.*): like this, that way

Holding his binoculars in his fist,
he said "Have <u>*a see*</u>, look here, *like this*."

mucho

MOO-cho (*adv.*): a lot, very much

Mike was a *moocher*, and he borrowed *a lot*;
his friends often gave him all that they'd got.

de vez en cuando

de ves en KWAN-do (*adv.*): occasionally

Devils in candor *occasionally* **speak;**
the tales that they tell would make your
knees really weak.

maravillosamente

ma-ra-vee-yo-sa-MEN-te (*adv.*): wonderfully

Mara's villas are meant to be exclusive; they're *wonderfully* luxurious and meant for the reclusive.

DRILL 21

Refresh Your Memory

Match the word and link to its corresponding definition.

1. sencillamente (send silly men tea)
2. difícilmente (difficult)
3. rápidamente (rapidly)
4. aquí (a key)
5. debajo (Deb)
6. mal (mall)
7. así (a see)
8. mucho (moocher)
9. de vez en cuando (devils in candor)
10. maravillosamente (Mara's villas are meant)

A. bad
B. like this, that way
C. underneath
D. hardly, scarcely; with difficulty
E. wonderfully
F. simple, in a straightforward manner
G. here
H. occasionally
I. quickly
J. a lot, very much

Test Your Knowledge

Fill in the blanks with the appropriate adverb.

1. La señora tenía mucha prisa. Corrió _____ al bus.

2. Es muy fácil cortar el césped: lo puedes hacer _____, pero toma mucho tiempo.

3. _____ están las llaves. Las dejaste sobre el armario.

4. Nos gusta _____ ir al cine: vamos todos los viernes.

5. Se sintió _____ cuando supo de la muerte de su vecina.

6. Encontramos el juguete _____ de la cuna.

7. _____ es Marta: curiosa e inteligente.

8. _____, preparo una paella. Generalmente no tengo la paciencia.

9. Este apartamento está decorado _____. Los dueños tienen muy buen gusto.

10. Las cucarachas son muy fuertes: mueren _____.

lentamente

leen-ta-MEN-te (*adv.*): slowly

After hours of debate, the tea-lending committee
slowly decreed that it would _lend the men tea_.

poco

PO–ko/a (*adv.*): a little

Paul likes _polka_ only *a little*
because sometimes he finds the rhythms
silly and brittle.

casi

KA-see (*adv.*): almost

The magician steps aside so that the audience *can see* the little rabbit in the hat is *almost* free.

ahora

a-O-ra (*adv.*): now

The mystic will *now* read <u>an aura</u>,
it glows around her client like a magical flora.

nunca

NOON-ka (adv.): never

Will school end at _noon_?
Never, not until the cow jumps over the moon.

a veces

a VE-ses *(adv.)*: **sometimes**

A vase is *sometimes* **broken**
when loud or unkind words are spoken.

encima [de]

en-SEE-ma de (*adv.*): above

Ants see Marty Day as a kind of god
because he towers five feet *above* the sod.

menos

ME-nos (*adv.*): less

The *mean nose* was *less* stressed
when his shirts were all pressed.

siempre

SYEM-pre (*adv.*): always

See them pray the modern way:
The nuns *always* kick up their heels
at the end of the day.

peor

pe-ORR (*adv.*): worse

Dinner that night was like a curse:
Peas or **broccoli, what could be** *worse*?

DRILL 22

Refresh Your Memory

Match the word and link to its corresponding definition.

1. lentamente (lend the men tea)
2. poco (polka)
3. casi (can see)
4. ahora (an aura)
5. nunca (noon)
6. a veces (a vase is)
7. encima de (ants see Marty Day)
8. menos (mean nose)
9. siempre (see them pray)
10. peor (peas or)

A. sometimes
B. worse
C. never
D. now
E. always
F. a little
G. slowly
H. less
I. almost
J. above

Test Your Knowledge

Fill in the blanks with the appropriate adverb.

1. _____ terminé de leer la revista. Me faltaban 10 páginas.

2. El gato se subió _____ la mesa.

3. ¿Quieres ir a la biblioteca _____ , o luego?

4. _____ hemos ido a Argentina. Quisiéramos ir alguna vez.

5. Tienes que tener mucho cuidado cuando cortas las uñas de un bebé: lo tienes que hacer muy _____.

6. La señora no cocina todos los días; _____ su marido la lleva a un restaurante.

7. Me gusta el jugo de naranja bastante; me gusta el jugo de toronja sólo un _____.

8. Este restaurante es malísimo, pero ese es aún _____.

9. Si tienes _____ de 10.000 pesos en tu cuenta, el banco te cobra una carga.

10. Cuando los señores Méndez van al teatro, _____ piden los mismos asientos. Son sus asientos favoritos.

cerca [de]

SER-ka (*adv.*): near, close to

**There is a high concentration of clowns
when you get *close* to the *Circus Day* grounds.**

lejos [de]

LE-hos (*adv.*): far from

**Something's wrong with Farmer _Lee's hose_;
it's too _far_ from the soil where his desert rose grows.**

entre

EN-tre (adv.): between

Between the curtains the young actress *entered*;
on her lovely face the spotlight was centered.

despúes [de]

de–SPWES (*adv.*): after

After failing the test,
he was sad and *depressed*.

antes [de]

AN-tes (*adv.*): before

**The great old _aunties_ told boring lore
about how life was *before* the war.**

allí

a-YEE **(*adv.*): over there**

Once <u>*a year*</u>, *over there*, by the big red chair,
Santa visits his elves in the North Pole square.

ya

ya (*adv.*): already

"<u>Yeah</u>, " said Madison, "I cleaned my room."
"I *already* did it—and I'll get to homework soon."

pronto

PRON-to/a *(adv.)*: soon

The famous soccer player's *pro toe*
would *soon* be recognized with a golden bow.

afuera

a-FWE-ra (*adv.*): outside

A fur-wearer stepped *outside* in her luxurious hide,
but activists taunted her as she took her first stride.

otra vez

O-tra ves (*adv.*): again

**The florist brought home a bouquet of roses *again*,
and put them in the *ultra-vase* in the den.**

DRILL 23

Refresh Your Memory

Match the word and link to its corresponding definition.

1. cerca [de] (Circus Day)
2. lejos [de] (Lee's hose)
3. entre (entered)
4. despúes [de] (depressed)
5. antes [de] (aunties)
6. allí (a year)
7. ya (yeah)
8. pronto (pro toe)
9. afuera (a fur-wearer)
10. otra vez (ultra-vase)

A. before
B. between
C. again
D. after
E. outside
F. far from
G. soon
H. over there
I. near, close to
J. already

Test Your Knowledge

Fill in the blanks with the appropriate adverb.

1. Asegúrate de cerrar con llave todas las puertas _____ de acostarte.

2. Sigue estos pasos: primero multiplica por seis, _____ resta tres.

3. La biblioteca está muy _____ la universidad: queda a menos de 100 metros.

4. La clase número 103 queda _____ las clases 103 y 104.

5. _____ está la pluma que buscabas.

6. ¿Terminaste de leer el libro? Sí, _____ terminé.

7. Vivo _____ mis padres. Yo vivo en Puerto Rico y ellos viven en México.

8. Se acerca el invierno: _____ hará mucho frío.

9. ¿Te gustó la canción que escribí? ¿La quieres escuchar _____?

10. Hace calor _____, pero adentro de la casa tenemos aire acondicionado.

hoy

oy (*adv.*): today

"*Oy* vey," the exasperated mothers say.
"Would you kids please stop complaining *today*?"

sí

see (*adv.*): yes

"Say *yes* if you can <u>see</u> me,"
said the imaginary friend to baby Mimi.

mientras

MYEN-tras (*adv.*): while

<u>*Men trust*</u> that *while* their wives are at the mall,
the amount of money they'll spend will be small.

donde

DON-de *(adv.)*: where

On the horizon, at the _dawn_ of the _day_,
is _where_ the two Eskimos will meet on their sleighs.

ayer

ai-ER (*adv.*): yesterday

Yesterday the scent of flowers filled the _air_;
today clouds are gray, and the pears feel despair.

cuándo

KWAN-do *(adv.)*: when

When Jeffrey earns his black belt in Tae *Kwon Do*,
he'll easily be able to defeat any foe.

entonces

en–TON–ses (*adv.*): then

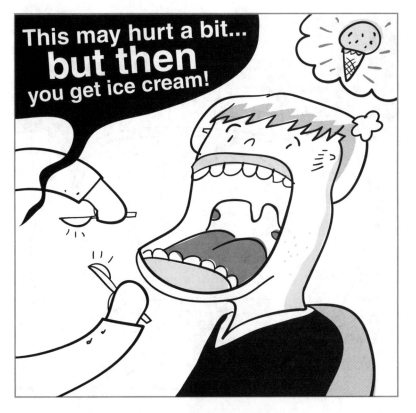

Getting out his *tonsils* made Tony want to scream;
then he heard he'd get to eat ice cream.

dentro

DEN-tro (*adv.*): inside, within, in

Dennis was no driving star:
He was so bad he got a _dent_ _inside_ his car.

abajo

a-BA-ho (*adv.*): below, underneath, down, downstairs

Old farmer Joe used _a bad hoe_;
he couldn't get to the rich earth just *below* the snow.

temprano

tem-PRA-no *(adv.)*: early

**Emma didn't like to wake up *early*,
and when the _temperature_ was low, she felt surly.**

DRILL 24

Refresh Your Memory

Match the word and link to its corresponding definition.

1. hoy (oy)
2. sí (see)
3. mientras (men trust)
4. donde (dawn ... day)
5. ayer (air)
6. cuándo (Kwon Do)
7. entonces (tonsils)
8. dentro (dent)
9. abajo (a bad hoe)
10. temprano (temperature)

A. where
B. today
C. inside, within, in
D. below, underneath, down, downstairs
E. yesterday
F. when
G. then
H. while
I. early
J. yes

Test Your Knowledge

Fill in the blanks with the appropriate adverb.

1. La cáscara de la manzana es roja, pero por _____ la fruta es blanca.

2. ¿Tienes hambre? _____, quisiera comer pronto.

3. _____ mi madre preparaba la cena, mi hermana ponía la mesa.

4. _____ fuimos al gimnasio: hoy nos duelen los músculos.

5. El libro está _____ lo dejaste: en el escritorio.

6. Cuando era pequeña vivíamos en Los Ángeles. _____ íbamos todos los días a la playa.

7. _____ tengo una cita con el peluquero a las tres.

8. La lavadora está _____, en el sótano.

9. ¿_____ termina el partido de fútbol?

10. La señora se levanta muy _____, a las cinco de la mañana.

detrás

de-TRAS (*adv.*): behind, in back of, after

The irresponsible hikers threw the _day's trash_ _behind_ them on the nature path.

mejor

me-HOR (*adv.*): better

Said the boastful director, after a round of encores, "*My horror* film is *better* than yours."

tampoco

tam-PO-ko (*adv.*): neither

We went over to *Tammi's poker* game,
but *neither* of us played as her hair was aflame.

arriba

a-REE-ba (*adv.*): above, up

The spotted frog let out _a ribbit_
as it leaped *above* to catch up with a tidbit.

también

tam-BYEN (*adv.*): also, too

When Shelley's jug band made its debut,
she sang harmonies and played the *tambourine*, *too*.

tarde

TAR-de (*adv.*): late

On the town's *tar day*, the mixing truck was *late*,
so the townspeople knew dirt roads were their fate.

bastante

ba–STAN-te *(adv.)*: enough

Sue had *enough* awards to display
so she threw her *Best Auntie* trophy away.

muy

mooy *(adv.)*: very

My boy is *very* environmentally aware;
he recycles his garbage, and his showers are rare.

como

KO-mo (*adv.*): as, like

The teacher's _comb over_ was *like* a big cresting wave;
it hung over the side of his head and didn't behave.

en frente de

en FREN-te de (*adv.*): across from

In front of the *deli*, *across from* the park,
the sweet-toothed girl waited for her chocolate bark.

DRILL 25

Refresh Your Memory

Match the word and link to its corresponding definition.

1. detrás (day's trash)
2. mejor (my horror)
3. tampoco (Tammi's poker)
4. arriba (a ribbit)
5. también (tambourine)
6. tarde (tar day)
7. bastante (Best Auntie)
8. muy (my boy)
9. como (comb over)
10. en frente de (in front ... deli)

A. very
B. enough
C. neither
D. late
E. better
F. also, too
G. behind, in back of, after
H. across from
I. above, up
J. as like

Test Your Knowledge

Fill in the blanks with the appropriate adverb.

1. Es _____ importante comer comida saludable.

2. La computadora nueva es _____ que la vieja.

3. Juan Carlos vive en el piso de _____.

4. Los hijos de Magdalena juegan al ajedrez; _____ juegan al back gamón.

5. No le gusta la comida japonesa; _____ le gusta la comida coreana.

6. Regresemos a casa. Se está haciendo _____.

7. Prepara la carne _____ quieras: con cebollas o con tomates.

8. El ladrón se estaba escondiendo _____ del carro.

9. Existen _____ razas de perros.

10. La niña se paró _____ espejo y admiró su disfraz.

Practice Drill Answers

Verbs

Drill 1, page 16
Refresh Your Memory: 1. E; 2. A; 3. G; 4. H; 5. C; 6. I; 7. B; 8. J; 9. F; 10. D

Test Your Knowledge: 1. espero; 2. dibujo; 3. tomaste; 4. regresasteis; 5. busca; 6. aprender; 7. estudiaste; 8. escribió; 9. crees; 10. vendió

Drill 2, page 27
Refresh Your Memory: 1. B; 2. H; 3. E; 4. I; 5. A; 6. J; 7. D; 8. C; 9. G; 10. F

Test Your Knowledge: 1. traigo; 2. miras; 3. vivió; 4. leyeron; 5. comimos; 6. pensáis; 7. entendisteis; 8. abro; 9. mienten; 10. pusiste

Drill 3, page 38
Refresh Your Memory: 1. H; 2. C; 3. F; 4. A; 5. D; 6. J; 7. I; 8. E; 9. B; 10. G

Test Your Knowledge: 1. diste; 2. lavaron; 3. dijo; 4. confío; 5. estamos; 6. salimos; 7. me desperté; 8. se bañaron; 9. es 10. levantar

Drill 4, page 49
Refresh your Memory: 1. H; 2. D; 3. B; 4. F; 5. A; 6. I; 7. G; 8. J.; 9. E; 10. C

Test Your Knowledge: 1. te atreves; 2. resfriarme; 3. se sentaron; 4. se asustó; 5. te enfadaste; 6. hablo; 7. se rió; 8. se casaron; 9. llega; 10. viajan

Drill 5, page 60
Refresh Your Memory: 1. B; 2. D; 3. F; 4. C; 5. A; 6. I; 7. H; 8. G; 9. E; 10. J

Test Your Knowledge: 1. hago; 2. fue; 3. conducir; 4. compró; 5. llevó; 6. tradujo; 7. sabe; 8. pido; 9. preguntasteis; 10. conoces

Drill 6, page 71
Refresh Your Memory: 1. A; 2. C; 3. I; 4. E; 5. B; 6. G; 7. D; 8. F; 9. J; 10. H

Test Your Knowledge: 1. corro; 2. tocas; 3. empezó; 4. rompió; 5. sacamos; 6. venís; 7. regar; 8. tuvo; 9. viste; 10. juegan

Drill 7, page 82
Refresh Your Memory: 1. E; 2. G; 3. C; 4. I; 5. B; 6. J; 7. A; 8. D; 9. H; 10. F

Test Your Knowledge: 1. ganamos; 2. volvió; 3. escoger; 4. enseñó; 5. compartir; 6. gustan; 7. perdí; 8. cierra; 9. lloró; 10. olvida

Drill 8, page 93
Refresh Your Memory: 1. I; 2. J; 3. F; 4. B; 5. D; 6. A; 7. H; 8. C; 9. G; 10. E

Test Your Knowledge: 1. asistió; 2. puedo; 3. cantó; 4. dormí; 5. odio; 6. quiso; 7. cuentas; 8. mostró; 9. aman; 10. recuerdas

Drill 9, page 104

Refresh Your Memory: 1. E; 2. B; 3. G; 4. J; 5. H; 6. C; 7. A; 8. I; 9. D; 10. F

Test Your Knowledge: 1. montan; 2. sonrió; 3. escuchaste; 4. se vistió; 5. contestar; 6. subir; 7. barre; 8. soñé; 9. sorprendimos; 10. beber

Drill 10, page 115

Refresh Your Memory: 1. D; 2. A; 3. F; 4. I; 5. H; 6. B; 7. J; 8. C; 9. G; 10. E

Test Your Knowledge: 1. saltó; 2. seguir; 3. besó; 4. tire; 5. pintó; 6. debe; 7. descubrimos; 8. crecer; 9. prometo; 10. cortar

Drill 11, page 126

Refresh Your Memory: 1. F; 2. D; 3. J; 4. E; 5. C; 6. H; 7. A; 8. I; 9. G; 10. B

Test Your Knowledge: 1. te divertiste; 2. se preocupa; 3. huelen; 4. coser; 5. se ducharon; 6. cruzaron; 7. murió; 8. mandamos; 9. temo; 10. falta

Drill 12, page 137

Refresh Your Memory: 1. G; 2. D; 3. I; 4. H; 5. C; 6. A; 7. E; 8. J; 9. F; 10. B

Test Your Knowledge: 1. construyó; 2. volar; 3. oíste; 4. bailamos; 5. mezclas; 6. andar; 7. nació; 8. bromear; 9. permite; 10. limpiaron

Drill 13, page 148

Refresh Your Memory: 1. B; 2. F; 3. D; 4. H; 5. C; 6. G; 7. E; 8. J; 9. A; 10. I

Test Your Knowledge: 1. nadar; 2. se sintió; 3. cocinar; 4. abrazó; 5. ayudó;

6. hay; 7. dolió; 8. parar; 9. coce al horno; 10. planché

Drill 14, page 159

Refresh Your Memory: 1. D; 2. C; 3. F; 4. A; 5. H; 6. E; 7. B; 8. J; 9. G; 10. I

Test Your Knowledge: 1. calentamos; 2. se cayó; 3. cuelgas; 4. presté; 5. acostarme; 6. afeitarse; 7. se maquilló; 8. llamó; 9. llenar; 10. apoyas

Drill 15, page 170

Refresh Your Memory: 1. B; 2. H; 3. F; 4. D; 5. A; 6. G; 7. E; 8. J; 9. C; 10. I

Test Your Knowledge: 1. escondió; 2. se calla; 3. gastamos; 4. despegó; 5. lanzó; 6. patear; 7. derritió; 8. atar; 9. anular; 10. peinarme

Adjectives

Drill 16, page 182

Refresh Your Memory: 1. J; 2. E; 3. B; 4. A; 5. H; 6. F; 7. D; 8. I; 9. C; 10. G

Test Your Knowledge: 1. bueno; 2. antipática; 3. guapo; 4. baja; 5. aburrido; 6. gorda; 7. joven; 8. linda; 9. vieja; 10. habladora

Drill 17, page 193

Refresh Your Memory: 1. C; 2. F; 3. A; 4. G; 5. J; 6. B; 7. I; 8. H; 9. D; 10. E

Test Your Knowledge: 1. simpática; 2. grande; 3. pobre; 4. travieso; 5. pesado; 6. altos; 7. bonito; 8. pequeñas; 9. única; 10. delgada

Drill 18, page 204

Refresh Your Memory: 1. I; 2. G; 3. J; 4. D; 5. B; 6. E; 7. H; 8. C; 9. A; 10. F

Test Your Knowledge: 1. fría; 2. feo; 3. embarazada; 4. cara; 5. vacía; 6. triste; 7. ocupado/a; 8. sucio; 9. cansados; 10. feliz

Drill 19, page 215

Refresh Your Memory: 1. A; 2. D; 3. H; 4. F; 5. B; 6. J; 7. G; 8. I; 9. C; 10. E

Test Your Knowledge: 1. caliente; 2. rico; 3. enferma; 4. loco; 5. fastidioso; 6. nuevo; 7. tranquilo; 8. cómicos; 9. débil; 10. baratas

Drill 20, page 226

Refresh Your Memory: 1. C; 2. H; 3. B; 4. D; 5. F; 6. G; 7. A; 8. I; 9. J; 10. E

Test Your Knowledge: 1. torpes; 2. ruidosos; 3. estrecho; 4. mezquino; 5. gratis; 6. orgullosos; 7. fuerte; 8. claros; 9. perezoso; 10. verdaderos

Adverbs

Drill 21, page 238

Refresh Your Memory: 1. F; 2. D; 3. I; 4. G; 5. C; 6. A; 7. B; 8. J; 9. H; 10. E

Test Your Knowledge:
1. rápidamente; 2. sencillamente; 3. aquí; 4. mucho; 5. mal; 6. debajo; 7. así; 8. de vez en cuando; 9. maravillosamente; 10. difícilmente

Drill 22, page 249

Refresh Your Memory: 1. G; 2. F; 3. I; 4. D; 5. C; 6. A; 7. J; 8. H; 9. E; 10. B

Test Your Knowledge: 1. casi; 2. encima de; 3. ahora; 4. nunca; 5. lentamente; 6. a veces; 7. poco; 8. peor; 9. menos; 10. siempre

Drill 23, page 260

Refresh Your Memory: 1. I; 2. F; 3. B; 4. D; 5. A; 6. H; 7. J; 8. G; 9. E; 10. C

Test Your Knowledge: 1. antes de; 2. después; 3. cerca de; 4. entre; 5. allí; 6. ya; 7. lejos de; 8. pronto; 9. otra vez; 10. afuera

Drill 24, page 271

Refresh Your Memory: 1. B; 2. J; 3. H; 4. A; 5. E; 6. F; 7. G; 8. C; 9. D; 10. I

Test Your Knowledge: 1. dentro; 2. sí; 3. mientras; 4. ayer; 5. donde; 6. entonces; 7. hoy; 8. abajo; 9. cuándo; 10. temprano

Drill 25, page 282

Refresh Your Memory: 1. G; 2. E; 3. C; 4. I; 5. F; 6. D; 7. B; 8. A; 9. J; 10. H

Test Your Knowledge: 1. muy; 2. mejor; 3. arriba; 4. también; 5. tampoco; 6. tarde; 7. como; 8. detrás; 9. bastantes; 10. en frente de

Index

hablar, 48

hacer, 52

hoy, 261

ir, 51

joven, 178

jugar, 61

lanzar, 164

lavarse, 37

leer, 17

lejos, 251

lentamente, 239

levantar, 36

limpiar, 134

lindo, 177

llamar, 157

llenar, 158

llegar, 46

llevar, 57

llorar, 78

loco, 208

mal, 233

mandar, 123

maquillarse, 155

maravillosamente, 237

mejor, 273

menos, 246

mentir, 24

mezclar, 131

mezquino, 221

mientras, 263

mirar, 19

montar, 94

morir, 121

mostrar, 90

mucho, 235

muy, 279

nacer, 133

nadar, 138

nuevo, 210

nunca, 243

ocupado, 202

odiar, 87

oír, 128

oler, 119

olvidar, 80

orgulloso, 222

otra vez, 259

parar, 145

patear, 165

pedir, 58

perezoso, 225

preguntar, 59

peinarse, 168

pensar, 22

pequeño, 191

perder, 77

permitir, 135

peor, 248

pesado, 188

pintar, 110

planchar, 146

pobre, 183

poco, 240

poder, 83

poner, 26

prometer, 113

preocuparse, 116

prestar, 153

pronto, 257

querer, 89

rápidamente, 230

recorder, 91

regar, 66

regresar, 10

reírse, 45

resfriarse, 40

rico, 205

romperse, 65

ruidoso, 220

saber, 56

sacar, 63

salir, 28

saltar, 106

seguir, 105

sencillamente, 228

sentarse, 39

sentirse, 143

ser, 32

sí, 262

siempre, 247

simpático, 187

soñar, 102

sonreír, 96

sorprender, 101

subir, 98

sucio, 201

también, 276

tampoco, 274

tarde, 277

temer, 125

temprano, 270

tener, 67

tirar, 107

tocar, 62

tomar, 6

torpe, 218

traer, 25

traducir, 55

tranquilo, 207

travieso, 186

triste, 198

único, 184

vacío, 197

vender, 15

venir, 68

ver, 69

verdadero, 223

vestirse, 97

viajar, 47

viejo, 181

vivir, 21

volar, 136

volver, 79

ya, 256

About the Authors

Frances Duncan and **Dan O. Williams** are both artists and writers, as their projects and whims dictate. In this case, Frances wrote the words and Dan drew the cartoons. It could easily have been reversed. They are the proud parents of a lazy marshmallow-colored Labrador retriever, and they live in northwestern Massachusetts.